HOW TO KNOW
THE WILD
FLOWERS

HOW TO KNOW
THE WILD
FLOWERS

*A Guide
to The Names,
Haunts, and Habits of
Our Common Wild Flowers*

by

MRS. WILLIAM STARR DANA

Illustrated by
MARION SATTERLEE

With 25 New Paintings by
MANABU C. SAITO

Houghton Mifflin Company
BOSTON

Copyright © 1989 by Houghton Mifflin Company
Paintings copyright © 1989 by Manabu C. Saito

For information about permission to reproduce selections
from this book, write to Permissions, Houghton Mifflin
Company, 2 Park Street, Boston, Massachusetts 02108.

Library of Congress Cataloging-in-Publication Data

Parsons, Frances Theodora, 1861–1952.
How to know the wild flowers : a guide to the names, haunts,
and habits of our common wild flowers / by Mrs. William Starr
Dana ; illustrated by Marion Satterlee ; with 25 new paintings by
Manabu C. Saito.
P. cm.
Originally published: New York : Scribner, 1893.
Includes index.
ISBN 0-395-52103-3
ISBN 0-395-58565-1 (pbk.)
1. Wild flowers — Northeastern States —
Identification.   2. Wild flowers — Northeastern States —
Pictorial works.   I. Title.
QK118.P24   1989
582.13'0974 — dc20   89-11085
CIP

Printed in the United States of America

J 10 9 8 7 6 5 4 3 2

How to Know the Wild Flowers was first published
in 1893 by Charles Scribner's Sons.

CONTENTS

EDITOR'S NOTE

Almost a hundred years ago, Mrs. William Starr Dana wrote *How to Know the Wild Flowers,* a forerunner of our modern field guides and a book that would become an American classic. First published in 1893 by Charles Scribner's Sons, the book was an instant success; the first printing sold out in five days. The text was revised and enlarged in 1895 and again in 1900; in 1921 the publisher added some undistinguished color plates. The last printing of the cloth edition was in 1940.

Although largely forgotten today, Mrs. Dana's book is as fresh and lively as when it was first published. And while it has been supplanted as an identification guide by more complete and authoritative volumes, no contemporary guide can compare with *How to Know the Wild Flowers* for the richness, flavor, and sheer entertainment of Mrs. Dana's commentaries. It is not likely, for example, that we will look at a wood anemone, or windflower, again without remembering what Mrs. Dana wrote about the plant. After introducing the flower with a stanza from William Cullen Bryant and a line from Whittier, she continues:

> Pliny tells us that the anemone of the classics was so entitled because it opened at the wind's bidding. The Greek tradition claims that it sprang from the passionate tears shed by Venus over the body of the slain Adonis. At one time it was believed that the wind which passed over a field of anemones was poisoned, and that disease followed in its wake. Perhaps be-

cause of this superstition the flower was adopted as the emblem of illness by the Persians. . . .

On her own, Mrs. Dana was a shrewd, amusing observer of nature. Among the "cranks of the vegetable kingdom," she rates the evening primrose, which opens at night; the closed gentian, which never opens at all; and the wild ginger, which hides its flower head on the ground. Describing the way English ladies wore Queen Anne's lace flowers in their hair in place of feathers, she observes, "One can picture the dejected appearance of a ball-room belle at the close of an entertainment."

The poets and writers of her own day — Thoreau, Bryant, Emerson, Whittier, Longfellow, and others — are much in evidence. So, too, are glimpses of the life of a young girl in the nineteenth century. Of boneset she writes with obvious aversion:

> To one whose childhood was passed in the country some fifty years ago the name or sight of this plant is fraught with unpleasant memories. The attic or wood-shed was hung with bunches of the dried herb, which served as so many grewsome warnings against wet feet, or any over-exposure which might result in cold or malaria. A certain Nemesis, in the shape of a nauseous draught which was poured down the throat under the name of "boneset tea," attended such a catastrophe.

Frances Theodora Smith Dana Parsons was born in 1861 and brought up in New York City. She developed her love for nature during summers spent with her grandmother in Newburgh, New York, along the Hudson River. She was married at an early age to Commodore William Starr Dana, a naval officer considerably older than herself. She lost her first baby, and soon after, her husband died during an influenza epidemic in Paris.

As an escape from her sorrow and the draconian rules of Victorian mourning — which dictated not only dress but associates and appropriate activities — Mrs. Dana, enticed by her friend Marion Satterlee, began taking walks and resumed her childhood interest in plants and flowers. Although the late nineteenth century saw the beginnings of the conservation movement and a popular interest in nature, the only source of information about flowers was in technical tomes like Gray's *Manual of Botany*. About this time, Mrs. Dana read a magazine article by the naturalist John Burroughs, which was the direct inspiration for her book. "Some of these days," Burroughs wrote,

> someone will give us a handbook of our flowers, by the aid of which we shall all be able to name those we gather on our walks without the trouble of analyzing them. In this book we shall have a list of all our flowers arranged according to color, as white flowers, blue flowers, yellow flowers, red flowers, etc., with the place of growth and the time of blooming.

In addition to *How to Know the Wild Flowers*, Mrs. Dana published *According to the Seasons*, a collection of essays about wildflowers that first appeared in the *New York Tribune*. She also wrote a botany book for children.

During the early years of her second marriage, when her husband, James Russell Parsons, Jr., had financial problems, she wrote a companion volume to her wildflower book, *How to Know the Ferns*. After publishing four books in six years, the last in 1899, Mrs. Parsons gave up writing. She became a campaign worker in the suffrage movement and later moved into Republican state politics. Her privately printed autobiography, *Perchance Some Day*, published in 1951, a year before her death, portrays a way of life common among the eastern aristocracy — she was an intimate of the Roosevelt family — and tells stories of the political intrigues that went on in New York State Republican circles.

In this new edition of *How to Know the Wild Flowers*, some of Mrs. Dana's briefer entries have been dropped and the botanical and common names have been updated. The original line drawings have been retained (although the color plates added in 1921 have not), and the beautiful turn-of-the-century binding by designer Margaret

Armstrong has been reproduced. The twenty-five new color plates were commissioned from Manabu C. Saito, an artist noted for his exquisite flower paintings.

FRANCES TENENBAUM
Boston 1989

LIST OF COLOR
ꟷ ILLUSTRATIONS ꟷ

PREFACE TO THE
⚙ FIRST EDITION ⚙

The pleasure of a walk in the woods and fields is enhanced a hundredfold by some little knowledge of the flowers which we meet at every turn. Their names alone serve as a clew to their entire histories, giving us that sense of companionship with our surroundings which is so necessary to the full enjoyment of outdoor life. But if we have never studied botany it has been no easy matter to learn these names, for we find that the very people who have always lived among the flowers are often ignorant of even their common titles, and frequently increase our eventual confusion by naming them incorrectly. While it is more than probable that any attempt to attain our end by means of some "Key," which positively bristles with technical terms and outlandish titles, has only led us to replace the volume in despair, sighing, with Emerson, that these scholars

> "Love not the flower they pluck, and know it not,
>   And all their botany is Latin names!"

So we have ventured to hope that such a book as this will not be altogether unwelcome, and that our readers will find that even a bowing acquaintance with the flowers repays one generously for the effort expended in its achievement. Such an acquaintance serves to transmute the tedium of a railway journey into the excitement of a tour of discovery. It causes the monotony of a drive through an ordinarily uninteresting country to be forgotten in the diversion of noting the wayside flowers, and counting a hundred different species where formerly less than a dozen would have been detected.

It invests each boggy meadow and bit of rocky woodland with almost irresistible charm. Surely Sir John Lubbock is right in maintaining that "those who love nature can never be dull," provided that love be expressed by an intelligent interest rather than by a purely sentimental rapture.

The "Flower Descriptions" should be consulted in order to learn the actual dimensions of the different plants, as it has not always been possible to preserve their relative sizes in the illustrations. The aim in the drawings has been to help the reader to identify the flowers described in the text, and to this end they are presented as simply as possible, with no attempt at artistic arrangement or grouping.

New York, March 15, 1893.

"Most young people find botany a dull study. So it is, as taught from the text-books in the schools; but study it yourself in the fields and woods, and you will find it a source of perennial delight."

JOHN BURROUGHS

INTRODUCTORY

∿ CHAPTER ∿

Until a comparatively recent period the interest in plants centred largely in the medicinal properties, and sometimes in the supernatural powers, which were attributed to them.

> "—O who can tell
> The hidden power of herbes and might of magick spell?—"

sang Spenser in the "Faerie Queen;" and to this day the names of many of our wayside plants bear witness, not alone to the healing properties which their owners were supposed to possess, but also to the firm hold which the so-called "doctrine of signatures" had upon the superstitious mind of the public. In an early work on "The Art of Simpling," by one William Coles, we read as follows: "Yet the mercy of God which is over all his works, maketh Grasse to grow upon the Mountains and Herbes for the use of men, and hath not only stamped upon them a distinct forme, but also given them particular signatures, whereby a man may read, even in legible characters, the use of them." Our hepatica or liverleaf, owes both its generic and English titles to its leaves, which suggested the form of the organ after which the plant is named, and caused it to be considered "a sovereign remedy against the heat and inflammation of the liver."*

Although his once-renowned system of classification has since been discarded on account of its artificial character, it is probably

---

*Henry Lyte (1529–1607), an English herbalist.

to Linnaeus* that the honor is due of having raised the study of plants to a rank which had never before been accorded it. The Swedish naturalist contrived to inspire his disciples with an enthusiasm, and to invest the flowers with a charm and personality which awakened a wide-spread interest in the subject. It is only since his day that the unscientific nature-lover, wandering through those woods and fields where

> "— wide around, the marriage of the plants
> Is sweetly solemnized —"

has marvelled to find the same laws in vogue in the floral as in the animal world.

To Darwin we owe our knowledge of the significance of color, form, and fragrance in flowers. These subjects have been widely discussed during the last twenty-five years, because of their close connection with the theory of natural selection; they have also been more or less enlarged upon in modern text-books. Nevertheless, it seems wiser to repeat what is perhaps already known to the reader, and to allude to some of the interesting theories connected with these topics, rather than to incur the risk of obscurity by omitting all explanation of facts and deductions to which it is frequently necessary to refer.

It is agreed that the object of a flower's life is the making of seed, *i.e.*, the continuance of its kind. Consequently its most essential parts are its reproductive organs, the stamens, and the pistil or pistils.

The stamens are the fertilizing organs. These produce the powdery, quickening material called pollen, in little sacs which are borne at the tips of their slender stalks.

The pistil is the seed-bearing organ. The pollen-grains which are deposited on its roughened summit throw out minute tubes which penetrate the style, reaching the little ovules in the ovary below, and quickening them into life.

These two kinds of organs can easily be distinguished in any

---

*Carolus Linnaeus (1707–1778), the Swedish botanist who devised the binomial taxonomic system.

large, simple, complete flower. The pollen of the stamens, and the ovules which line the base of the pistil, can also be detected with the aid of an ordinary magnifying-glass.

Now, we have been shown that nature apparently prefers that the pistil of a flower should not receive its pollen from the stamens in the same flower-cup with itself. Experience teaches that sometimes when this happens no seeds result. At other times the seeds appear, but they are less healthy and vigorous than those which are the outcome of *cross-fertilization* — the term used by botanists to describe the quickening of the ovules in one blossom by the pollen from another.

But perhaps we hardly realize the importance of abundant health and vigor in a plant's offspring.

Let us suppose that our eyes are so keen as to enable us to note the different seeds which, during one summer, seek to secure a foothold in some few square inches of the sheltered roadside. The neighboring herb-roberts and jewelweeds discharge — catapult fashion — several small invaders into the very heart of the little territory. A battalion of silky-tufted seeds from the cracked pods of the milkweed float downward and take lazy possession of the soil, while the heavy rains wash into their immediate vicinity those of the violet from the overhanging bank. The hooked fruit of the sticktight is finally brushed from the hair of some exasperated animal by the jagged branches of the neighboring thicket and is deposited on the disputed ground, while a bird passing just overhead drops earthward the seed of the partridgeberry. The ammunition of the witch hazel, too, is shot into the midst of this growing colony; to say nothing of a myriad more little squatters that are wafted or washed or dropped or flung upon this one bit of earth, which is thus transformed into a bloodless battle-ground, and which is incapable of yielding nourishment to one-half or one-tenth or even one hundredth of these tiny strugglers for life!

So, to avoid diminishing the vigor of their progeny by *self-fertilization* (the reverse of cross-fertilization), various species take various precautions. In one species the pistil is so placed that the pollen of the neighboring stamens cannot reach it. In others one of these two organs ripens before the other, with the result that the contact of the pollen with the stigma of the pistil would be ineffectual. Often the stamens and pistils are in different flowers, sometimes on different plants. But these pistils must, if possible, receive the necessary pollen in some way and fulfil their destiny by setting seed. And we have been shown that frequently it is brought to them by insects, occasionally by birds, and that sometimes it is blown to them by the winds.

Ingenious devices are resorted to in order to secure these desirable results. Many flowers make themselves useful to the insect world by secreting somewhere within their dainty cups little glands of honey, or, more properly speaking, nectar, for honey is the result of the bees' work. This nectar is highly prized by the insects, and is in many cases the only object which attracts them to the flowers, although sometimes the pollen, which Darwin believes to have been the only inducement offered formerly, is sought as well.

But of course this nectar fails to induce visits unless the bee's attention is first attracted to the blossom, and it is tempted to explore the premises; and we now observe the interesting fact that those flowers which depend upon insect-agency for their pollen, usually advertise their whereabouts by wearing bright colors or by exhaling fragrance. It will also be noticed that a flower sufficiently conspicuous to arrest attention by its appearance alone is rarely fragrant.

When, attracted by either of these significant characteristics — color or fragrance — the bee alights upon the blossom, it is sometimes guided to the very spot where the nectar lies hidden by markings of some vivid color. Thrusting its head into the heart of the flower for the purpose of extracting the secret treasure, it unconsciously strikes the stamens with sufficient force to cause them to powder its body with pollen. Soon it flies away to another plant *of the same kind,* where, in repeating the process just described, it unwittingly brushes some of the pollen from the first blossom upon the pistil of the second, where it helps to make new seeds. Thus these busy bees which hum so restlessly through the long summer days are working better than they know and are accomplishing more important feats than the mere honey-making which we usually associate with their ceaseless activity.

Those flowers which are dependent upon night-flying insects for their pollen contrive to make themselves noticeable by wearing white or pale yellow — red, blue, and pink being with difficulty detected in the darkness. They, too, frequently indicate their presence by exhaling perfume, which in many cases increases in intensity as the night falls and a clew to their whereabouts becomes momentarily more necessary. This fact partially accounts for the large proportion of fragrant white flowers. Darwin found that the proportion of sweet-scented white flowers to sweet-scented red ones was 14.6 per cent. of white to 8.2 of red.

We notice also that some of these night-fertilized flowers close during the day, thus insuring themselves against the visits of insects which might rob them of their nectar or pollen, and yet be unfitted by the shape of their bodies to accomplish their fertilization. On the other hand, many blossoms which are dependent upon the sun-loving bees close at night, securing the same advantage.

Then there are flowers which close in the shade, others at the approach of a storm, thus protecting their pollen and nectar from the dissolving rain; others at the same time every day. Linnaeus invented a famous "flower-clock," which indicated the hours of the day by the closing of different flowers. This habit of closing has been called the "sleep of flowers."

There is one far from pleasing class of flowers which entices insect-visitors — not by attractive colors and alluring fragrance — but "by deceiving flies through their resemblance to putrid meat — imitating the lurid appearance as well as the noisome smell of carrion." Our common carrion-flower, which covers the thickets so profusely in early summer that Thoreau complained that every bush and copse near the river emitted an odor which led one to imagine that all the dead dogs in the neighborhood had drifted to its shore, is probably an example of this class, without lurid color, but certainly with a sufficiently noisome smell! Yet this foul odor seems to answer the plant's purpose as well as their delicious aroma does that of more refined blossoms, if the numberless small flies which it manages to attract are fitted to successfully transmit its pollen.

Certain flowers are obviously adapted to the visits of insects by their irregular forms. The fringed or otherwise conspicuous lip and long nectar-bearing spur of many orchids point to their probable dependence upon insect agency for perpetuation; while the papilionaceous blossoms of the Pea family also betray interesting adaptations for cross-fertilization by the same means. Indeed it is believed that irregularity of form is rarely conspicuous in a blossom that is not visited by insects.

The position of a nodding flower, like the harebell, protects its pollen and nectar from the rain and dew; while the hairs in the throat of many blossoms answer the same purpose and exclude useless insects as well.

Another class of flowers which calls for special mention is that which is dependent upon the wind for its pollen. It is interesting to observe that this group expends little effort in useless adornment. "The wind bloweth where it listeth" and takes no note of form or color. So here we find those

"Wan flowers without a name,"

which, unheeded, line the way-side. The common plantain of the country dooryard, from whose long tremulous stamens the light, dry pollen is easily blown, is a familiar example of this usually ignored class. Darwin first observed, that "when a flower is fertilized by the wind it never has a gayly colored corolla." Fragrance and nectar as well are usually denied these sombre blossoms. Such is the occasional economy of that at times most reckless of all spendthrifts — nature!

Some plants — certain violets and the jewelweeds among others — bear small inconspicuous blossoms which depend upon no outside agency for fertilization. These never open, thus effectually guarding their pollen from the possibility of being blown away by the wind, dissolved by the rain, or stolen by insects. They are called *cleistogamous* flowers.

Nature's clever devices for securing a wide dispersion of seeds have been already hinted at. One is tempted to dwell at length upon the ingenious mechanism of the elastically bursting capsules of one species, and the deft adjustment of the silky sails which waft the seeds of others; on the barbed fruits which have pressed the most unwilling into their prickly service, and the bright berries which so temptingly invite the hungry winter birds to peck at them till their precious contents are released, or to devour them, digesting only the pulpy covering and allowing the seeds to escape uninjured into the earth at some conveniently remote spot.

Then one would like to pause long enough to note the slow movements of the climbing plants and the uncanny ways of the insect-devourers. At our very feet lie wonders for whose elucidation a lifetime would be far too short. Yet if we study for ourselves the mysteries of the flowers, and, when daunted, seek their interpretation in those devoted students who have made this task part of their life-work, we may hope finally to attain at least a partial insight into those charmed lives which find

"— tongues in trees, books in the running brooks,
Sermons in stones, and good in everything."

I

WHITE

BLOODROOT *Sanguinaria canadensis*

BLOODROOT.

Sanguinaria canadensis. Poppy Family.

Rootstock. — Thick; charged with a crimson juice. *Leaves.* —
Rounded; deeply lobed. *Flower.* — White; terminal.

In early April the curled-up leaf of the bloodroot, wrapped in
its papery bracts, pushes its firm tip through the earth and brown
leaves, bearing within its carefully shielded burden, the young erect
flower-bud. When the perils of the way are passed and a safe height
is reached, this pale, deeply lobed leaf resigns its precious charge
and gradually unfolds itself; meanwhile the bud slowly swells into
a blossom.

Surely no flower of the year can vie with this in spotless beauty.
Its very transitoriness enhances its charm. The snowy petals fall
from about their golden centre before one has had time to grow
satiated with their perfection. Unless the rocky hillsides and wood-
borders are jealously watched it may escape us altogether. One or
two warm sunny days will hasten it to maturity, and a few more
hours of wind and storm shatter its loveliness.

Care should be taken in picking the flower — if it must be
picked — as the red liquid which oozes blood-like from the
wounded stem makes a lasting stain. This crimson juice was prized
by the Indians as a decoration for their faces and tomahawks.

SHADBUSH. JUNEBERRY. SERVICEBERRY.

Amelanchier canadensis. Rose Family.

A tall shrub or small tree found in low ground. *Leaves.* — Oblong;
acutely pointed; finely toothed; mostly rounded at base. *Flowers.* —
White; growing in racemes. *Fruit.* — Round; red; sweet and edible;
ripening in June.

Down in the boggy meadow, in early March, we can almost
fancy that from beneath the solemn purple cowls of the skunk-
cabbage brotherhood comes the joyful chorus —

3

"For lo, the winter is past!"

but we chilly mortals still find the wind so frosty and the woods so unpromising that we return shivering to the fireside, and refuse to take up the glad strain till the feathery clusters of the shadbush droop from the pasture thicket. Then only are we ready to admit that

"The flowers appear upon the earth,
The time of the singing of birds is come."

Even then, search the woods as we may, we shall hardly find thus early in April another shrub in blossom, unless it be the spicebush, whose tiny honey-yellow flowers escape all but the careful observer. The shadbush has been thus named because of its flowering at the season when shad "run;" Juneberry, because the shrub's crimson fruit surprises us by gleaming from the copses at the very beginning of summer; serviceberry, because of the use made by the Indians of this fruit, which they gathered in great quantities, and, after much crushing and pounding, made into a sort of cake.

WOOD ANEMONE. WINDFLOWER.

Anemone quinquefolia. Buttercup Family.

Stem. — Slender. *Leaves.* — Divided into delicate leaflets. *Flower.* — Solitary; white, pink, or purplish.

"— Within the woods,
Whose young and half transparent leaves scarce cast
A shade, gay circles of anemones
Danced on their stalks;"

writes Bryant, bringing vividly before us the feathery foliage of the spring woods, and the tremulous beauty of the slender-stemmed anemones. Whittier, too, tells how these

"— wind-flowers sway
Against the throbbing heart of May."

And in the writings of the ancients as well we could find many allusions to the same flower, were we justified in believing that the blossom christened the "wind-shaken," by some poet flower-lover of early Greece, was identical with our modern anemone.

Pliny tells us that the anemone of the classics was so entitled because it opened at the wind's bidding. The Greek tradition claims that it sprang from the passionate tears shed by Venus over the body of the slain Adonis. At one time it was believed that the wind which had passed over a field of anemones was poisoned, and that disease followed in its wake. Perhaps because of this superstition the flower was adopted as the emblem of illness by the Persians. Surely our delicate blossom is far removed from any suggestion of disease or unwholesomeness, seeming instead to hold the very essence of spring and purity in its quivering cup.

WOOD ANEMONE *Anemone quinquefolia*

RUE-ANEMONE.

Anemonella thalictroides. Buttercup Family.

Stem. — Six to twelve inches high. *Leaves.* — Divided into rounded leaflets. *Flowers.* — White or pinkish; clustered.

The rue-anemone seems to linger especially about the spreading roots of old trees. It blossoms with the wood anemone, from which it differs in bearing its flowers in clusters.

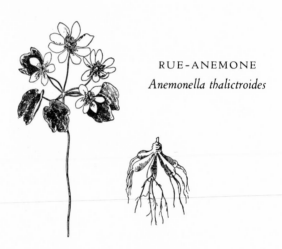

RUE-ANEMONE
Anemonella thalictroides

Red Trillium
Trillium erectum
(page 210)

Yellow Adder's-Tongue
Erythronium americanum
(page 92)

Spring-Beauty
Claytonia virginica
(page 157)

Bloodroot
Sanguinaria canadensis
(page 3)

Skunk Cabbage
Symplocarpus foetidus
(page 270)

Wood Anemone
Anemone quinquefolia
(page 4)

Round-lobed Hepatica
Hepatica americana
(page 227)

Trailing Arbutus
Epigaea repens
(page 155)

EARLY SPRING

GOLDTHREAD.

Coptis groenlandica. Buttercup Family.

Scape. — Slender; three to five inches high. *Leaves.* — Evergreen; shining; divided into three leaflets. *Flowers.* — White; solitary. *Root.* — Of long, bright yellow fibres.

This decorative little plant abundantly carpets the northern bogs and extends southward over the mountains. Its delicate flowers appear in May, but its shining, evergreen leaves are noticeable throughout the year. The bright yellow thread-like roots give it its common name.

STARFLOWER.

Trientalis borealis. Primrose Family.

Stem. — Smooth; erect. *Leaves.* — Thin; pointed; whorled at the summit of the stem. *Flowers.* — White; delicate; star-shaped.

Finding this delicate flower in the May woods, one is at once reminded of the anemone. The whole effect of plant, leaf, and snow-white blossom is starry and pointed. The frosted tapering petals distinguish it from the rounded blossoms of the wild strawberry, near which it often grows.

STARFLOWER *Trientalis borealis*

9

CANADA MAYFLOWER.
WILD LILY-OF-THE-VALLEY.

Maianthemum canadense. Lily Family.

Stem. — Three to six inches high; with two or three leaves. *Leaves.* — Lance-shaped to oval; heart-shaped at base. *Flowers.* — White or straw-color; growing in a raceme. *Fruit.* — A red berry.

This familiar and pretty little plant, long without any homely English name, is now known as "Canada Mayflower," but while undoubtedly it grows in Canada and flowers in May, the name is not a happy one, for it abounds as far south as North Carolina, and is not the first blossom to be entitled "Mayflower."

In late summer the red berries are often found in close proximity to the fruit of the shinleaf and pipsissewa.

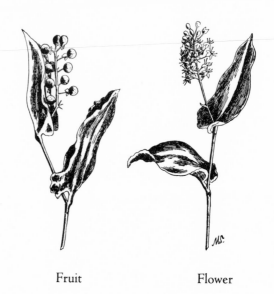

Fruit   Flower

CANADA MAYFLOWER *Maianthemum canadense*

EARLY SAXIFRAGE.

Saxifraga virginiensis. Saxifrage Family.

Scape. — Four to nine inches high. *Leaves.* — Clustered at the root; somewhat wedge-shaped; narrowed into a broad leaf-stalk. *Flowers.* — White; small; clustered.

In April we notice that the seams in the rocky cliffs and hillsides begin to whiten with the blossoms of the early saxifrage. *Steinbrech* — stonebreak — the Germans appropriately entitle this little plant, which bursts into bloom from the minute clefts in the rocks and which has been supposed to cause their disintegration by its growth. The generic and common names are from *saxum* — a rock, and *frangere* — to break.

EARLY SAXIFRAGE *Saxifraga virginiensis*

WATERCRESS.

Nasturtium officinale. Mustard Family.

Leaves. — Divided into roundish segments. *Flowers.* — White, clustered.

Although the watercress is not a native of North America it has made itself so entirely at home in many of our streams that we hardly look upon it as a stranger. Whoever, after a long ramble through the woods on a summer morning, has plucked its fresh, pungent leaves from some sparkling stream and added them to his frugal sandwich, looks upon the little plant with a sense of familiar gratitude, which we rarely feel toward an alien.

The name *nasturtium*, signifying twisted nose, is said to be given to this genus on account of the effect supposedly produced on the nose by eating the acrid leaves.

MAY-APPLE. MANDRAKE.

Podophyllum peltatum. Barberry Family.

Flowering-stem. — Two-leaved; one-flowered. *Flowerless-stems.* — Terminated by one large, rounded, much-lobed leaf. *Leaves* (of flowering-stems). — One-sided; five to nine-lobed, the lobes oblong; the leaf-stalks fastened to their lower side near the inner edge. *Flower.* — White; large; nodding from the fork made by the two leaves. *Fruit.* — A large, fleshy, egg-shaped berry.

"The umbrellas are out!" cry the children, when the great green leaves of the May-apple first unfold themselves in spring. These curious-looking leaves at once betray the hiding-place of the pretty, but, at times, unpleasantly odoriferous flower which nods beneath them. They lie thickly along the woods and meadows in many parts of the country, arresting one's attention by the railways. The fruit, which ripens in July, has been given the name of "wild lemon," in some places on account of its shape. It was valued by the Indians for medicinal purposes, and its mawkish flavor still seems to find favor with the children, notwithstanding its frequently unpleasant after-effects. The leaves and roots are poisonous if taken internally, and are said to have been used as a pot herb, with fatal results. They yield an extract which has been utilized in medicine.

Fruit

MAY-APPLE *Podophyllum peltatum*

DUTCHMAN'S-BREECHES. WHITE-HEARTS.

Dicentra cucullaria. Poppy Family.

Scape. — Slender. *Leaves.* — Thrice-compound. *Flowers.* — White and yellow; growing in a raceme.

There is something singularly fragile and spring-like in the appearance of this plant as its heart-shaped blossoms nod from the rocky ledges where they thrive best. One would suppose that the firmly closed petals guarded against any intrusion on the part of

Tuberous rootstocks

DUTCHMAN'S-BREECHES *Dicentra cucullaria*

insect-visitors and indicated the flower's capacity for self-fertilization; but it is found that when insects are excluded by means of gauze no seeds are set, which goes to prove that the pollen from another flower is a necessary factor in the continuance of this species. The generic name, *Dicentra*, is from the Greek and signifies *two-spurred*. The flower, when seen, explains its two English titles. It is accessible to every New Yorker, for in early April it whitens many of the shaded ledges in the upper part of the Central Park.

SQUIRREL-CORN.
Dicentra canadensis. Poppy Family.

The squirrel-corn closely resembles the Dutchman's-breeches. Its greenish or pinkish flowers are heart-shaped, with short, rounded spurs. They have the fragrance of hyacinths, and are found blossoming in early spring in the rich woods of the North.

CREEPING SNOWBERRY.
Gaultheria hispidula. Heath Family.

Stem. — Slender; trailing and creeping. *Leaves.* — Evergreen; small; ovate; pointed. *Flowers.* — Small; white; solitary from the axils of the leaves. *Fruit.* — A pure white berry.

One must look in May for the flower of this plant; but it is late in the summer when the beautiful little creeper especially challenges our admiration. Studded with snow-white berries, it nearly covers some decaying log which has fallen into a lonely Adirondack stream. Or else it thickly carpets the peat-bog where we are hunting cranberries, or brightens the moist mossy woods which earlier in the year were redolent with the breath of the twin-flower. Its aromatic flavor suggests the wintergreen and sweet birch.

FOAMFLOWER. FALSE MITERWORT.

Tiarella cordifolia. Saxifrage Family.

Stem. — Five to twelve inches high; leafless, or rarely with one or two leaves. *Leaves.* — From the rootstock or runners; heart-shaped; sharply lobed. *Flowers.* — White; in a full raceme.

Over the hills and in the rocky woods of April and May the graceful white racemes of the foamflower arrest our attention. This is a near relative of the *Mitella* or true miterwort. Its generic name is a diminutive from the Greek for *turban,* and is said to refer to the shape of the pistil.

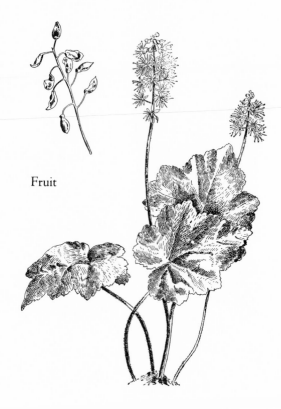

Fruit

FOAMFLOWER *Tiarella cordifolia*

WHITE TRILLIUM.

Trillium grandiflorum. Lily Family.

Stem. — Stout; from a tuber-like root stock. *Leaves.* — Ovate; three in a whorl, a short distance below the flower. *Flower.* — Single; terminal; large; white, turning pink or marked with green. *Fruit.* — A large ovate, somewhat angled, dark purple berry.

This singularly beautiful flower is found during April and May. Its great white stars gleam from shaded wood borders or from the banks of swift-flowing streams.

The nodding trillium, *T. cernuum,* bears its smaller white or pinkish blossom in a manner which suggests the may-apple, on a stalk so curved as sometimes quite to conceal the flower beneath the leaves. This is a fragrant and attractive blossom, which may be found in the early year in moist shaded places.

The painted trillium, *T. undulatum,* is also less large and showy than the great white trillium, but it is quite as pleasing. Its white petals are painted at their base with red stripes. This species is very plentiful in the Adirondack and Catskill Mountains.

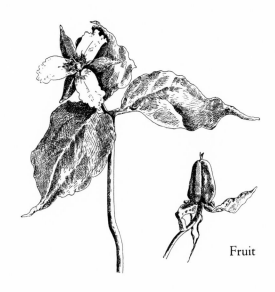

Fruit

PAINTED TRILLIUM *Trillium undulatum*

GINSENG.

Panax quinquefolius. Ginseng Family.

Root. — Large and spindle-shaped; often forked. *Stem.* — About one foot high. *Leaves.* — Three in a whorl; divided into leaflets. *Flowers.* — Greenish-white; in a simple umbel. *Fruit.* — Bright red; berry-like.

This plant is well known by name, but is yearly becoming more scarce. The aromatic root was so greatly valued in China for its supposed power of combating fatigue and old age that it could only be gathered by order of the emperor. The forked specimens were believed to be the most powerful, and their fancied likeness to the human form obtained for the plant the Chinese title of *Jin-chen* (from which ginseng is a corruption), and the Indian one of *Garantoguen*, both which, strangely enough, are said to signify, *like a man.* The Canadian Jesuits first began to ship the roots of the American species to China, where they sold at about five dollars a pound. In 1900 they commanded about one-fifth of that price in the home market.

Trumpet Honeysuckle
Lonicera sempervirens
(page 223)

May-Apple
Podophyllum peltatum
(page 12)

Mayweed
Anthemis cotula
(page 42)

Blazing-Star
Liatris spicata
(page 251)

Early Saxifrage
Saxifraga virginiensis
(page 11)

Goldthread
Coptis groenlandica
(page 9)

Bearberry
Arctostaphylos uva-ursi
(page 23)

Canada Mayflower
Maianthemum canadense
(page 10)

MAY

TOOTHWORT. PEPPERWORT.

Dentaria diphylla. Mustard Family.

Rootstock. — Five to ten inches long; wrinkled; crisp; of a pleasant, pungent taste. *Stem.* — Leafless below; bearing two leaves above. *Leaves.* — Divided into three toothed leaflets. *Flowers.* — White; in a terminal cluster.

The toothwort has been valued, not so much on account of its pretty flowers which may be found in the rich May woods, but for its crisp, edible root, which has lent savor to many a simple luncheon in the cool shadows of the forest.

TOOTHWORT *Dentaria diphylla*

DWARF GINSENG. GROUNDNUT.

Panax trifolius. Ginseng Family.

Stem. — Four to eight inches high. *Leaves.* — Three in a whorl; divided into from three to five leaflets. *Flowers.* — White; in an umbel. *Fruit.* — Yellowish; berry-like. *Root.* — A globular tuber.

The tiny white flowers of the dwarf ginseng are so closely clustered as to make "one feathery ball of bloom," to quote Mr. Hamilton Gibson.* This little plant resembles its larger relative the true ginseng. It blossoms in our rich open woods early in spring, and hides its small round tuber so deep in the earth that it requires no little care to uproot it without breaking the slender stem. This tuber is edible and pungent tasting, giving the plant its name of groundnut.

CANADA VIOLET.

Viola canadensis. Violet Family.

Stem. — Leafy; upright; one to two feet high. *Leaves.* — Heart-shaped; pointed; toothed. *Flowers.* — White, veined with purple, violet beneath, otherwise greatly resembling the common blue violet.

We associate the violet with the early year, but I have found the delicate fragrant flowers of this species blossoming high up on the Catskill Mountains late into September; and have known them to continue to appear in a New York city-garden into November. They are among the loveliest of the family, having a certain sprightly self-assertion which is peculiarly charming, perhaps because so unexpected.

The tiny sweet white violet, *V. blanda,* with brown or purple veins, which is found in nearly all low, wet, woody places in spring,

---

*William Hamilton Gibson, an American painter and writer who specialized in botany (1850–1896).

is perhaps the only uniformly fragrant member of the family, and its scent, though sweet, is faint and elusive.

The lance-leaved violet, *V. lanceolata*, is another white species which is easily distinguished by its smooth lance-shaped leaves, quite unlike those of the common violet. It is found in damp soil, especially eastward.

CANADA VIOLET *Viola canadensis*

BEARBERRY.

Arctostaphylos uva-ursi. Heath Family.

A trailing shrub. *Leaves.* — Thick and evergreen; smooth; somewhat wedge-shaped. *Flowers.* — Whitish; clustered.

This plant blossoms in May or June, and is found on rocky hillsides or in sandy soil. Its name refers to the relish with which bears are supposed to devour its fruit.

RED OSIER.

Cornus stolonifera. Dogwood Family.

A shrub from three to six feet high. *Branches* (especially the young shoots). — Bright purplish-red. *Leaves.* — Ovate; rounded at base; short-pointed; roughish; whitish beneath. *Flowers.* — White; small; in flat clusters. *Fruit.* — White or lead-color.

This is a common shrub in wet places, especially northward, flowering in June or early July; being easily identified throughout the year by its bright reddish branches, and after midsummer by its conspicuous lead-colored berries.

FALSE SOLOMON'S-SEAL.

Smilacina racemosa. Lily Family.

Stems. —Usually curving; one to three feet long. *Leaves.* — Oblong; veiny. *Flowers.* — Greenish-white; small; in a terminal raceme. *Fruit.* — A pale red berry speckled with purple.

A singular lack of imagination is betrayed in the common name of this plant. Despite a general resemblance to the true Solomon's-seal, and the close proximity in which the two are constantly found, *S. racemosa* has enough originality to deserve an individual title. The position of the much smaller flowers is markedly different. Instead of drooping beneath the stem they terminate it, having frequently a pleasant fragrance, while the berries of late summer are pale red, flecked with purple. It puzzles one to understand why these two plants should so constantly be found growing side by side — so close at times that they almost appear to spring from one point. The generic name is from *smilax,* on account of a supposed resemblance between the leaves of this plant and those which belong to that genus.

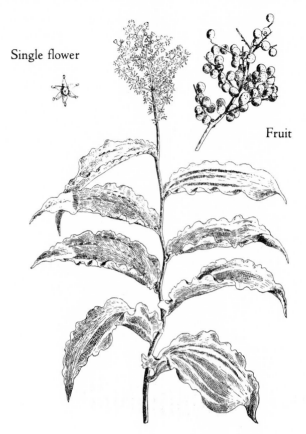

Single flower

Fruit

FALSE SOLOMON'S-SEAL *Smilacina racemosa*

WHITE BANEBERRY.

Actaea pachypoda. Buttercup Family.

Stem. — About two feet high. *Leaves.* — Twice or thrice-compound; leaflets incised and sharply toothed. *Flowers.* — Small; white; in a thick, oblong, terminal raceme. *Fruit.* — An oval white berry, with a dark spot, on a *thick red stalk,* growing in a cluster.

The feathery clusters of the white baneberry may be gathered when we go to the woods for the columbine, the wild ginger, the

Jack-in-the-Pulpit, and Solomon's-seal. These flowers are very nearly contemporaneous and seek the same cool shaded nooks, all often being found within a few feet of one another.

The red baneberry, *A. rubra,* is a somewhat more northern plant and usually blossoms a week or two earlier. Its cherry-red (occasionally white) berries on their *slender stalks* are easily distinguished from the white ones of *A. pachypoda,* which look strikingly like the china eyes that small children occasionally manage to gouge from their dolls' heads.

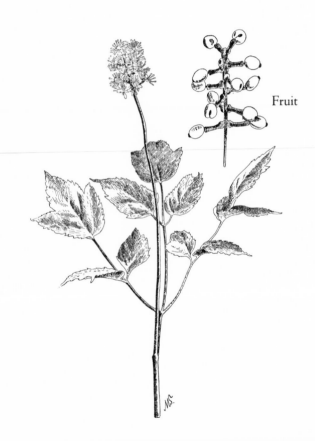

Fruit

WHITE BANEBERRY *Actaea pachypoda*

BUNCHBERRY. DWARF CORNEL.

Cornus canadensis. Dogwood Family.

Stem. — Five to seven inches high. *Leaves.* — Ovate; pointed; the upper crowded into an apparent whorl of four to six. *Flowers.* — Greenish; small; in a cluster which is surrounded by a large and showy four-leaved, petal-like white or pinkish involucre. *Fruit.* — Bright red; berry-like.

When one's eye first falls upon the pretty flowers of the bunchberry in the June woods, the impression is received that each low stem bears upon its summit a single large white blossom. A more searching look discovers that what appeared like rounded petals are really the showy white leaves of the involucre which surround the small, closely clustered, greenish flowers.

The bright red berries which appear in late summer make brilliant patches in the woods and swamps. Occasionally the plant is found flowering also at this season, its white stars showing to peculiar advantage among the little clusters of coral-like fruit. It is closely allied to the well-known flowering dogwood, which is so ornamental a tree in early spring.

In the Scotch Highlands it is called the "plant of gluttony," on account of its supposed power of increasing the appetite. It is said to form part of the winter food of the Esquimaux.

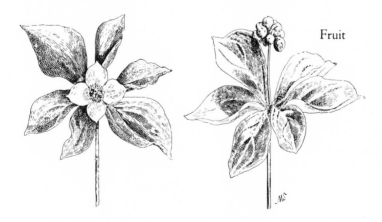

Fruit

BUNCHBERRY *Cornus canadensis*

WILD CALLA. WATER-ARUM.

Calla palustris. Arum Family.

Leaves. — Long-stemmed; heart-shaped. *Apparent Flower.* — Large; white. *Actual Flowers.* — Small; greenish; packed about the oblong spadix.

Although only eight or ten inches high, this plant is peculiarly striking as it rises from the rich soil of the swamp, or from the shallow borders of the stream. The broad smooth leaves at once remind one of its relationship to the so-called "calla-lily" of the greenhouses, a native of the Cape of Good Hope; and the likeness is still more apparent in the white, petal-like (although flat and open) spathe which tops the scape; so that even one knowing nothing of botanical families would naturally christen the plant "wild calla." The first sight of these white spathes gleaming across a wet meadow in June, and the closer inspection of the upright, vigorous little plants, make an event in the summer. None of our aquatics is more curious and interesting, more sturdy, yet dainty and pure, than the wild calla.

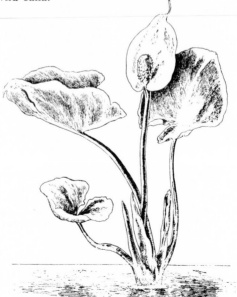

WILD CALLA *Calla palustris*

WINTERGREEN. CHECKERBERRY. MOUNTAIN-TEA.

Gaultheria procumbens. Heath Family.

Stem. — Three to six inches high; slender; leafy at the summit. *Leaves.* — Oval; shining; evergreen. *Flowers.* — White, growing from the axils of the leaves. *Fruit.* — A globular red berry.

He who seeks the cool shade of the evergreens on a hot July day is likely to discover the nodding wax-like flowers of this little plant. They are delicate and pretty, with a background of shining leaves. These leaves when young have a pleasant aromatic flavor similar to that of the sweet birch; they are sometimes used as a substitute for tea. The bright red berries are also edible and savory, and are much appreciated by the hungry birds and deer during the winter. If not thus consumed they remain upon the plant until the following spring, when they either drop or rot upon the stem, thus allowing the seeds to escape.

Fruit

WINTERGREEN *Gaultheria procumbens*

SWAMP-HONEYSUCKLE. CLAMMY AZALEA.

Rhododendron viscosum. Heath Family.

A shrub from three to ten feet high. *Leaves.* — Oblong. *Flowers.*—
White; clustered; appearing after the leaves.

The fragrant white flowers of this beautiful shrub appear in early
summer along the swamps which skirt the coast, and occasionally
farther inland. The close family resemblance to the pink azalea
(page 179) will be at once detected. On the branches of both species will be found those abnormal fleshy growths, called variously
"swamp apples" and "May apples," which are so relished by the
children. Formerly these growths were attributed to the sting of an
insect, as in the "oak apple;" now they are generally believed to be
modified buds.

Shadbush
Amelanchier canadensis
(page 3)

Pink Azalea
Rhododendron nudiflorum
(page 179)

Bluebells
Mertensia virginica
(page 266)

Toothwort
Dentaria diphylla
(page 21)

Bellwort
Uvularia perfoliata
(page 94)

Canada Violet
Viola canadensis
(page 22)

Lance-leaved Violet
Viola lanceolata
(page 23)

Gill-over-the-Ground
Glechoma hederacea
(page 229)

Sweet White Violet
Viola blanda
(page 22)

APRIL FLOWERS

ONE-FLOWERED WINTERGREEN.

Moneses uniflora. Wintergreen Family.

Stem. — Two to four inches high. *Leaves.* — Rounded; thin; veiny; toothed; from the roots. *Flower.* — White or rose-colored; solitary; half an inch broad.

This lovely little plant is found in flower in the deep pine woods of June or July. It has all the grace and delicacy of its kinsman, the shinleaf and pipsissewa, but, if possible, is even more daintily captivating. The generic name is from two Greek words signifying *single* and *delight,* in reference to the "beauty which is a joy" of the solitary flower, and betraying the always pleasing fact that the scientist who christened it was fully alive to its peculiar charm.

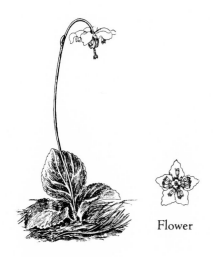

Flower

ONE-FLOWERED WINTERGREEN *Moneses uniflora*

MOUNTAIN LAUREL. CALICO-BUSH.

Kalmia latifolia. Heath Family.

An evergreen shrub. Leaves. — Oblong; pointed; shining; of a leathery texture. *Flowers.* — White or pink; in terminal clusters.

The shining green leaves which surround the white or rose-colored flowers of the mountain laurel are familiar to all who have skirted the west shore of the Hudson River, wandered across the hills that lie in its vicinity, or clambered across the mountains of Pennsylvania, where the shrub sometimes grows to a height of thirty feet. Not that these localities limit its range; for it abounds more or less from Canada to Florida, and far inland, especially along the mountains, whose sides are often clothed with an apparent mantle of pink snow during the month of June, and whose waste places are, in very truth, made to blossom like the rose at this season.

The ingenious contrivance of these flowers to secure cross-fertilization is most interesting. The long filaments of the stamens are arched by the fact that each anther is caught in a little pouch of the corolla; the disturbance caused by the sudden alighting of an insect on the blossom, or the quick brush of a bee's wing, dislodges the anthers from their niches, and the stamens spring upward with such violence that the pollen is jerked from its hiding-place in the pore of the anther-cell on to the body of the insect-visitor, who straightway carries it off to another flower upon whose protruding stigma it is sure to be inadvertently deposited. In order to see the working of this for one's self, it is only necessary to pick a fresh blossom and either brush the corolla quickly with one's finger, or touch the stamens suddenly with a pin, when the anthers will be dislodged and the pollen will be seen to fly.

This is not the laurel of the ancients — the symbol of victory and fame — notwithstanding some resemblance in the form of the leaves. The classic shrub is supposed to be identical with the *Laurus nobilis,* which was carried to our country by the early colonists, but which did not thrive in its new environment.

The leaves of our species are supposed to possess poisonous qualities, and are said to have been used by the Indians for suicidal purposes. There is also a popular belief that the flesh of a partridge which has fed upon its fruit becomes poisonous. The clammy exudation about the flower-stalks and blossoms may serve the purpose of excluding from the flower such small insects as would otherwise crawl up to it, dislodge the stamens, scatter the pollen, and yet be unable to carry it to its proper destination on the pistil of another flower.

The *Kalmia* was named by Linnaeus after Peter Kalm, one of his pupils who travelled in this country, who was, perhaps, the first to make known the shrub to his great master.

The title calico-bush probably arose from the marking of the corolla, which, to an imaginative mind, might suggest the cheap cotton-prints sold in the shops.

MOUNTAIN LAUREL
Kalmia latifolia

GREAT RHODODENDRON. GREAT LAUREL.

Rhododendron maximum. Heath Family.

A shrub from six to thirty-five feet high. *Leaves.* — Thick and leathery; oblong; entire. *Flowers.* — White or pink; clustered.

This beautiful native shrub is one of the glories of our country when in the perfection of its loveliness. The woods which nearly cover many of the mountains of our Eastern States hide from all but the bold explorer a radiant display during the early part of July. Then the lovely waxy flower-clusters of the American rhododendron are in their fulness of beauty. As in the laurel, the clammy

GREAT RHODODENDRON *Rhododendron maximum*

flower-stalks seem fitted to protect the blossom from the depredations of small and useless insects, while the markings on the corolla attract the attention of the desirable bee.

In those parts of the country where it flourishes most luxuriantly, veritable rhododendron jungles, termed "hells" by the mountaineers, are formed. The branches reach out and interlace in such a fashion as to be almost impassable.

The nectar secreted by the blossoms is popularly supposed to be poisonous. We read in Xenophon that during the retreat of the Ten Thousand the soldiers found a quantity of honey, of which they freely partook, with results that proved almost fatal. This honey is said to have been made from a rhododendron which is still common in Asia Minor, and which is believed to possess intoxicating and poisonous properties.

Comparatively little attention had been paid to this superb flower until the Centennial Celebration at Philadelphia, when some fine exhibits attracted the admiration of thousands. The shrub has been carefully cultivated in England, having been brought to great perfection on some of the English estates. It is yearly winning more notice in this country.

The generic name is from the Greek for *rose-tree*.

WOOD-SORREL.

Oxalis montana. Wood-sorrel Family.

Scape. — One-flowered; two to five inches high. *Leaves.* — Divided into three clover-like leaflets. *Flower.* — White, veined with red; solitary.

Surely nowhere can be found a daintier carpeting than that made by the clover-like foliage of the wood-sorrel, when studded with its rose-veined blossoms, in the northern woods of June. At the very name comes a vision of mossy nooks where the sunlight only comes on sufferance, piercing its difficult path through the tent-like foliage of the forest, resting only long enough to become a golden memory.

The early Italian painters availed themselves of its chaste beauty. Mr. Ruskin says: "Fra Angelico's use of the *Oxalis Acetosella* is as faithful in representation as touching in feeling. The triple leaf of the plant and white flower stained purple probably gave it strange typical interest among the Christian painters."

Throughout Europe it bears the odd name of "Hallelujah" on account of its flowering between Easter and Whitsuntide, the season when the Psalms sung in the churches resound with that word. There has been an unfounded theory that this title sprang from St. Patrick's endeavor to prove to his rude audience the possibility of a Trinity in Unity from the three-divided leaves. By many this ternate leaf has been considered the shamrock of the ancient Irish.

The English title, "cuckoo-bread," refers to the appearance of the blossoms at the season when the cry of the cuckoo is first heard.

Our name sorrel is from the Greek for *sour* and has reference to the acrid juice of the plant. The delicate leaflets "sleep" at night. That is, they droop and close one against another.

WOOD-SORREL *Oxalis montana*

SHINLEAF.

Pyrola elliptica. Wintergreen Family.

Stem. — Upright; scaly; terminating in a many-flowered raceme.
Leaves. — From the root; thin and dull; somewhat oval. *Flowers.* —
White; nodding.

In the distance these pretty flowers suggest the lilies-of-the-
valley. They are found in the woods of June and July, often in close
company with the pipsissewa. The ugly common name of shinleaf
arose from an early custom of applying the leaves of this genus to
bruises or sores; the English peasantry being in the habit of calling

SHINLEAF

Pyrola elliptica

any kind of plaster a "shin-plaster" without regard to the part of the body to which it might be applied. The old herbalist, Salmon,* says that the name *Pyrola* was given to the genus by the Romans on account of the fancied resemblance of its leaves and flowers to those of a pear-tree. The English also call the plant "wintergreen," which name we usually reserve for *Gaultheria procumbens.*

P. rotundifolia is a species with thick, shining, rounded leaves. It is the tallest of the genus, its scape standing, at times, one foot above the ground. This species exhibits several varieties with rose-colored flowers.

The smallest member of the group, *P. secunda,* is only from three to six inches high. Its numerous small, greenish flowers are turned to one side, and are scarcely nodding. They are clustered in spike-like fashion along the scape.

P. minor can be distinguished from all other *Pyrolas* by the short style which does not protrude from the globular blossom. This is a retiring little plant which is only found in our northern woods and mountains.

Many of these flowers are fragrant.

GRASS-OF-PARNASSUS.

Parnassia glauca. Saxifrage Family.

Stem. — Scape-like; nine inches to two feet high. *Leaves.* — Thickish; rounded; often heart-shaped; from the root. *Flower.* — White or cream-color; veiny.

Gerard** indignantly declares that this plant has been described by blind men, not "such as are blinde in their eyes, but in their understandings, for if this plant be a kind of grasse then may the

---

*William Salmon, an Englishman whose herbal, *Botanologia,* was published in 1710.
**John Gerard, an eminent sixteenth-century English botanist.

Butter-burre or Colte's-foote be reckoned for grasses — as also all other plants whatsoever." But if it covered Parnassus with its delicate veiny blossoms as abundantly as it does some moist New England meadows each autumn, the ancients may have reasoned that a plant almost as common as grass must somehow partake of its nature. The slender-stemmed creamy flowers are never seen to better advantage than when disputing with the fringed gentian the possession of some luxurious swamp.

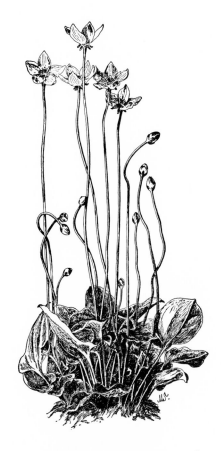

GRASS-OF-PARNASSUS *Parnassia glauca*

MAYWEED. CHAMOMILE.

Anthemis cotula. Composite Family.

Stem. — Branching. *Leaves.* — Finely dissected. *Flower-heads.* — Composed of white ray and yellow disk-flowers, resembling the common white daisy.

In midsummer the pretty daisy-like blossoms of this strong-scented plant are massed along the roadsides. So nearly a counter-part of the common daisy do they appear that they are constantly mistaken for that flower. The smaller heads, with the yellow disk-flowers crowded upon a receptacle which is much more conical than that of the daisy, and the finely dissected, feathery leaves, serve to identify the mayweed. The country-folk brew "chamomile tea" from these leaves, and through their agency raise painfully effective blisters in an emergency.

Celandine-Poppy
Stylophorum diphyllum
(page 98)

Twisted-Stalk
Streptopus roseus
(page 160)

Trillium
Trillium grandiflorum
(page 17)

Foamflower
Tiarella cordifolia
(page 16)

Celandine
Chelidonium majus
(page 98)

Perfoliate Bellwort
Uvularia perfoliata
(page 94)

Rue-Anemone
Anemonella thalictroides
(page 6)

Bluets
Houstonia caerulea
(page 227)

Spring-Beauty
Claytonia virginica
(page 157)

Dwarf Ginseng
Panax trifolius
(page 22)

LATE SPRING

PIPSISSEWA. PRINCE'S PINE.

Chimaphila umbellata. Wintergreen Family.

Stem. — Four to ten inches high; leafy. *Leaves.* — Somewhat whorled or scattered; evergreen; lance-shaped; with sharply toothed edges. *Flowers.* — White or pinkish; fragrant; in a loose terminal cluster.

When strolling through the woods in summer one is apt to chance upon great patches of these deliciously fragrant and pretty flowers. The little plant, with its shining evergreen foliage, flourishes abundantly among decaying leaves in sandy soil, and puts forth its dainty blossoms late in June. It is one of the latest of the fragile wood-flowers which are so charming in the earlier year, and which have already begun to surrender in favor of their hardier, more self-assertive brethren of the fields and roadsides. The common name, pipsissewa, is evidently of Indian origin.

PIPSISSEWA   *Chimaphila umbellata*

BLACK COHOSH. BUGBANE.
BLACK SNAKEROOT.

Cimicifuga racemosa. Buttercup Family.

Stem. — Three to eight feet high. *Leaves.* — Divided, the leaflets toothed or incised. *Flowers.* — White; growing in elongated wand-like racemes.

The tall white wands of the black cohosh shoot up in the shadowy woods of midsummer like so many ghosts. A curious-looking plant it is, bearing aloft the feathery flowers which have such an unpleasant odor that even the insects are supposed to avoid them. Fortunately they are sufficiently conspicuous to be admired at a distance, many a newly cleared hill-side and wood-border being lightened by their slender, torch-like racemes which flash upon us as we travel through the country. The plant was one of the many which the Indians believed to be efficacious for snake-bites. The generic name is from *cimex* — a bug, and *fugare* — to drive away.

INDIAN-PIPE. CORPSE-PLANT.

Monotropa uniflora. Wintergreen Family.

A low fleshy herb from three to eight inches high; without green foliage; of a wax-like appearance; with colorless bracts in the place of leaves. *Flower.* — White or pinkish; single; terminal; nodding.

"In shining groups, each stem a pearly ray,
      Weird flecks of light within the shadowed wood,
      They dwell aloof, a spotless sisterhood.
      No Angelus, except the wild bird's lay,
Awakes these forest nuns; yet, night and day,
      Their heads are bent, as if in prayerful mood.
      A touch will mar their snow, and tempests rude
      Defile; but in the mist fresh blossoms stray
From spirit-gardens, just beyond our ken.
      Each year we seek their virgin haunts, to look
      Upon new loveliness, and watch again

Their shy devotions near the singing brook;
Then, mingling in the dizzy stir of men,
Forget the vows made in that cloistered nook."*

The effect of a cluster of these nodding, wax-like flowers in the deep woods of summer is singularly fairy-like. They spring from a ball of matted rootlets, and are parasitic, drawing their nourishment from decaying vegetable matter. In fruit the plant erects itself and loses its striking resemblance to a pipe. Its clammy touch, and its disposition to decompose and turn black when handled, has earned it the name of corpse-plant. It was used by the Indians as an eye-lotion, and is still believed by some to possess healing properties.

*Mary Thacher Higginson, an American poet (1844–1941).

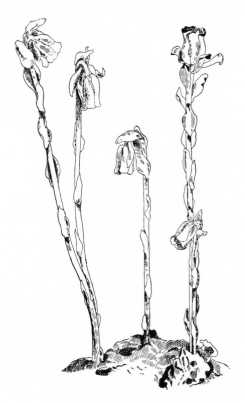

INDIAN-PIPE *Monotropa uniflora*

ENCHANTER'S NIGHTSHADE.

Circaea quadrisulcata. Evening-primrose Family.

Stem. — One or two feet high. *Leaves.* — Opposite; thin; ovate; slightly toothed. *Flowers.* — Dull white; small; growing in a raceme. *Fruit.* — Small; bur-like; bristly with hooked hairs.

This insignificant and ordinarily uninteresting plant arrests attention by the frequency with which it is found flowering in the summer woods and along shady roadsides.

C. *alpina* is a smaller, less common species, which is found along the mountains and in deep woods. Both species are burdened with the singularly inappropriate name of enchanter's nightshade. There is nothing in their appearance to suggest an enchanter or any of

ENCHANTER'S NIGHTSHADE *Circaea quadrisulcata*

the nightshades. It seems, however, that the name of a plant called after the enchantress Circe, and described by Dioscorides nearly two thousand years ago, was accidentally transferred to this unpretentious genus.

DEWDROP. ROBIN-RUN-AWAY.

Dalibarda repens. Rose Family.

Scape. — Low. *Leaves.* — Heart-shaped; wavy-toothed. *Flowers.* — White; one or two borne on each scape.

The foliage of this pretty little plant suggests the violet; while its white blossom betrays its kinship with the wild strawberry. It may be found from June till September in woody places, being one of those flowers which we seek deliberately, whose charm is never decreased by its being thrust upon us inopportunely. Who can tell how much the attractiveness of the wild carrot, the dandelion, or butter-and-eggs would be enhanced were they so discreet as to withdraw from the common haunts of men into the shady exclusiveness which causes us to prize many far less beautiful flowers?

DEWDROP *Dalibarda repens*

WHITE DAISY. WHITEWEED. OX-EYE DAISY.

Chrysanthemum leucanthemum. Composite Family.

The common white daisy stars the June meadows with those gold-centred blossoms which delight the eyes of the beauty-lover while they make sore the heart of the farmer, for the "whiteweed," as he calls it, is hurtful to pasture land and difficult to eradicate.

The true daisy is the *Bellis perennis* of England, — the

"Wee, modest crimson-tippit flower"

of Burns. This was first called "day's eye," because it closed at night and opened at dawn, —

"That well by reason men it call may,
The Daisie, or else the eye of the day,"

sang Chaucer nearly five hundred years ago. In England our flower is called "ox-eye" and "moon daisy;" in Scotland, "dog-daisy."

The plant is not native to this country, but was brought from the Old World by the early colonists.

Red Osier
Spreading Dogbane
Cornus stolonifera
Apocynum androsaemifolium
(page 24)
Yellow Loosestrife
(page 185)
Lysimachia terrestris
Bush-Honeysuckle
(page 106)
Diervilla lonicera
Whorled Loosestrife
(page 126)
Lysimachia quadrifolia
India Cucumber-Root
(page 105)
Medeola virginiana
Painted-Cup
(page 108)
Castilleja coccinea
Yellow Stargrass
(page 212)
Hypoxis hirsuta
(page 118)

Fringed Polygala
Large Cranberry
Polygala paucifolia
Vaccinium macrocarpon
(page 170)
(page 174)
EARLY SUMMER

THIMBLEWEED.

Anemone virginiana. Buttercup Family.

Stem. — Two or three feet high. *Leaves.* — Twice or thrice cleft, the divisions again toothed or cleft. *Flowers.* — Greenish or sometimes white; borne on long, upright flower-stalks.

These greenish flowers, which may be found in the woods and meadows throughout the summer, are chiefly striking by reason of their long, erect flower-stalks. The oblong, thimble-like fruit-head, which is very noticeable in the later year, gives to the plant its common name.

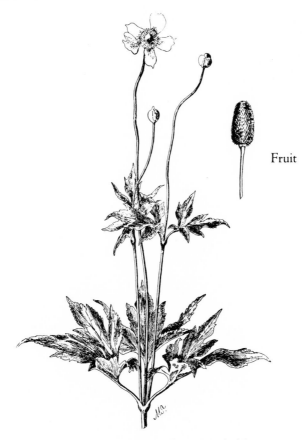

Fruit

THIMBLEWEED *Anemone virginiana*

PARTRIDGEBERRY.

Mitchella repens. Bedstraw Family.

Stems. — Smooth and trailing. *Leaves.* — Rounded; evergreen; veined with white. *Flowers.* — White or pinkish; fragrant; in pairs.

At all times of the year this little evergreen plant fulfils its mission of adorning that small portion of the earth to which it finds itself rooted. But only the early summer finds the partridgeberry exhaling its delicious fragrance from the delicate sister blossoms which are its glory. Among the waxy flowers will be found as many of the bright red berries of the previous year as have been left unmolested by the hungry winter birds. This plant is found not only in the moist woods of North America, but also in the forests of Mexico and Japan. It is a near relative of the dainty bluets or Quaker ladies, and has the same peculiarity of dimorphous flowers.

PARTRIDGEBERRY *Mitchella repens*

BUTTONBUSH.

Cephalanthus occidentalis. Bedstraw Family.

A shrub three to eight feet high. *Leaves.* — Opposite or whorled in threes; somewhat oblong and pointed. *Flowers.* — Small; white; closely crowded in round button-like heads.

This pretty shrub borders the streams and swamps throughout the country. Its button-like flower-clusters appear in midsummer. It belongs to the family of which the delicate bluet and fragrant partridgeberry are also members. Its flowers have a jasmine-like fragrance.

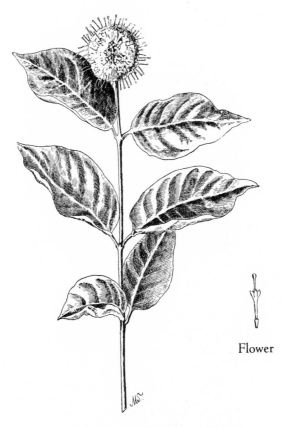

Flower

BUTTONBUSH *Cephalanthus occidentalis*

ROUND-LEAVED SUNDEW.

Drosera rotundifolia. Sundew Family.

Scape. — A few inches high. *Leaves.* — Rounded, abruptly narrowed into spreading, hairy leaf-stalks; beset with reddish, gland-bearing bristles. *Flowers.* — White; growing in a one-sided raceme, which so nods at its apex that the fresh-blown blossom is always uppermost.

> "What's this I hear
> About the new carnivora?
> Can little plants
> Eat bugs and ants
> And gnats and flies?
> A sort of retrograding:
> Surely the fare
> Of flowers is air,
> Or sunshine sweet;
> They shouldn't eat,
> Or do aught so degrading!"

But by degrees we are learning to reconcile ourselves to the fact that the more we study the plants the less we are able to attribute to them altogether unfamiliar and ethereal habits. We find that the laws which control their being are strangely suggestive of those which regulate ours, and after the disappearance of the shock which attends the shattered illusion, their charm is only increased by the new sense of kinship.

The round-leaved sundew is found blossoming in many of our marshes in midsummer. When the sun shines upon its leaves they look as though covered with sparkling dewdrops, hence its common name. These drops are a glutinous exudation, by means of which insects visiting the plant are first captured; the reddish bristles then close tightly about them, and it is supposed that their juices are absorbed by the plant. At all events the rash visitor rarely escapes. In many localities it is easy to secure any number of these little plants and to try for one's self the rather grewsome experiment of feeding them with small insects. Should the tender-hearted recoil from such reckless slaughter, they might confine their offerings on the altar of science to mosquitoes, small spiders, and other deservedly unpopular creatures.

The dew-thread, *D. filiformis*, has fine, thread-like leaves and pink flowers, and is found in wet sand along the coast.

> "A little marsh-plant, yellow green,
> And pricked at lip with tender red.
> Tread close, and either way you tread
> Some faint black water jets between
> Lest you should bruise the curious head.
>
> .   .   .
>
> You call it sundew: how it grows,
> If with its color it have breath,
> If life taste sweet to it, if death
> Pain its soft petal, no man knows:
> Man has no sight or sense that saith."
>
> —SWINBURNE.

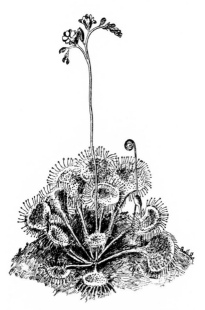

ROUND-LEAVED SUNDEW *Drosera rotundifolia*

POKEWEED. GARGET. PIGEONBERRY.

Phytolacca americana. Pokeweed Family.

Stems. — At length from six to ten feet high; purple-pink or bright red; stout. *Leaves.* — Large; alternate; veiny. *Flowers.* — White or pinkish. *Fruit.* — A dark purplish berry.

There is a vigor about this native plant which is very pleasing. In July it is possible that we barely notice the white flowers and large leaves; but when in September the tall purple stems rear themselves above their neighbors in the roadside thicket, the leaves look as though stained with wine, and the long clusters of rich dark berries hang heavily from the branches, we cannot but admire its independent beauty. The berries serve as food for the birds. A tincture of them at one time acquired some reputation as a remedy for rheumatism. In Pennsylvania they have been used with whiskey

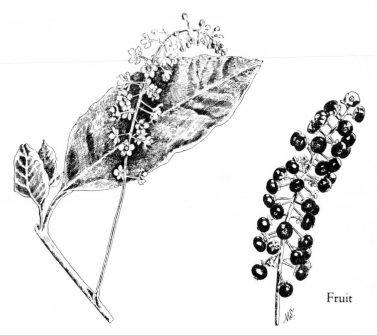

Fruit

POKEWEED *Phytolacca americana*

to make a so-called "port-wine." From their dark juice arose the name of "red-ink plant," which is common in some places. The large roots are poisonous, but the acrid young shoots are rendered harmless by boiling, and are eaten like asparagus, being quite as good, I have been told by country people.

Despite the difference in the spelling of the names, it has been suggested that the plant was called after President Polk. This is most improbable, as it was common throughout the country long before his birth, and its twigs are said to have been plucked and worn by his followers during his campaign for the presidency.

SWEET EVERLASTING. CATFOOT.

Gnaphalium obtusifolium. Composite Family.

Stem. — Erect; one to three feet high; woolly. *Leaves.* — Lance-shaped. *Flower-heads.* — Yellowish-white; clustered at the summit of the branches, composed of many tubular flowers.

This is the "fragrant life-everlasting," as Thoreau calls it, of late summer. It abounds in rocky pastures and throughout the some-what open woods.

WHITE SWEET CLOVER. WHITE MELILOT.

Melilotus alba. Pea Family.

Stem. — Two to four feet high. *Leaves.* — Divided into three-toothed leaflets. *Flowers.* — White; growing in spike-like racemes.

Like its yellow sister, *M. officinalis,* this plant is found blossoming along the roadsides throughout the summer. The flowers are said to serve as flavoring in Gruyère cheese, snuff, and smoking-tobacco, and to act like camphor when packed with furs to preserve them from moths, besides imparting a pleasant fragrance.

MEADOWSWEET.

Spiraea latifolia. Rose Family.

Stem. — Nearly smooth; two or three feet high. *Leaves.* — Alternate; very broadly lance-shaped; toothed. *Flowers.* — Small; white or flesh-color; in pyramidal clusters.

The feathery spires of the meadowsweet soar upward from the river banks and low meadows from July onward. Unlike its pink sister, the steeplebush, its leaves and stems are fairly smooth. The lack of fragrance in the flowers is disappointing, because of the hopes raised by the plant's common name. This is said by Dr. Prior* to be a corruption of the Anglo-Saxon *meadwort,* which signifies *honey-wine herb,* alluding to a fact which is mentioned in Hill's "Herbal,"** that "the flowers mixed with mead give it the flavor of the Greek wines."

Although the significance of many of the plant-names seems clear enough at first sight, such an example as this serves to show how really obscure it often is.

RATTLESNAKE-PLANTAIN.

Goodyera pubescens. Orchid Family.

Scape. — Six to twelve inches high. *Leaves.* — From the root in a sort of flat rosette; conspicuously veined with white; thickish; evergreen. *Flowers.* — Small; greenish-white; crowded in a close spike.

The flowers of the rattlesnake-plantain appear in late summer and are less conspicuous than the prettily tufted, white-veined leaves which may be found in the rich woods throughout the year. The plant has been reputed an infallible cure for hydrophobia and snake-bites. It is said that the Indians had such faith in its remedial

---

*Richard Chandler Alexander Prior (1809–1902), an English physician whose *Popular Names of British Plants* was first published in 1863.
**Sir John Hill, an eighteenth-century herbalist and apothecary.

MEADOWSWEET
Spiraea latifolia

RATTLESNAKE-PLANTAIN
Goodyera pubescens

virtues that they would allow a snake to drive its fangs into them for a small sum, if they had these leaves on hand to apply to the wound.

CULVER'S-ROOT.

Veronicastrum virginicum. Snapdragon Family.

Stem. — Straight and tall; from two to six feet high. *Leaves.* — Whorled; lance-shaped; finely toothed. *Flowers.* — White; small; growing in slender clustered spikes.

The tall straight stems of the culver's-root lift their slender spikes in midsummer to a height that seems strangely at variance with the habit of this genus. The small flowers, however, at once betray their kinship with the speedwells. Although it is, perhaps, a little late to look for the white wands of the black cohosh, the two plants might easily be confused in the distance, as they have much the same aspect and seek alike the cool recesses of the woods. This same species grows in Japan and was introduced into English gardens nearly two hundred years ago. It is one of the many Indian remedies which were adopted by our forefathers.

Swamp-Honeysuckle *Rhododendron viscosum* (page 30)	Water-Parsnip *Sium suave* (page 69)	Common Elder *Sambucus canadensis* (page 66)
Buttonbush *Cephalanthus occidentalis* (page 55)		Spotted Joe-Pye-Weed *Eupatorium maculatum* (page 193)
Rattlesnake-Weed *Hieracium venosum* (page 119)	Culver's-Root *Veronicastrum virginicum* (page 62)	Sticktight *Bidens frondosa* (page 134)

COUNTRY LANES

DAISY FLEABANE. SWEET SCABIOUS.

Erigeron annuus. Composite Family.

Stem. — Stout; from three to five feet high; branched; hairy. *Leaves.* — Coarsely and sharply toothed; the lowest ovate, the upper narrower. *Flower-heads.* — Small; clustered; composed of both ray and disk-flowers, the former white, purplish, or pinkish, the latter yellow.

During the summer months the fields and waysides are whitened with these very common flowers which look somewhat like small white daisies or asters.

Another common species is *E. strigosus,* a smaller plant, with smaller flower-heads also, but with the white ray-flowers longer. The generic name is from two Greek words signifying *spring* and *an old man,* in allusion to the hoariness of certain species which flower in the spring. The fleabanes were so named from the belief that when burned they were objectionable to insects. They were formerly hung in country cottages for the purpose of excluding such unpleasant intruders.

PEARLY EVERLASTING.

Anaphalis margaritacea. Composite Family.

Stem. — Erect; one or two feet high. *Leaves.* — Broadly linear to lance-shaped. *Flower-heads.* — Composed entirely of tubular flowers with very numerous white involucral scales.

This species is common throughout our northern woods and pastures, blossoming in August. Thoreau writes of it in September: "The pearly everlasting is an interesting white at present. Though the stems and leaves are still green, it is dry and unwithering, like an artificial flower; its white, flexuous stem and branches, too, like wire wound with cotton. Neither is there any scent to betray it. Its amaranthine quality is instead of high color. Its very brown centre now affects me as a fresh and original color. It monopolizes small circles in the midst of sweet fern, perchance, on a dry hill-side."

COMMON ELDER.

Sambucus canadensis. Honeysuckle Family.

Stems. — Scarcely woody; five to ten feet high. *Leaves.* — Divided into toothed leaflets. *Flowers.* — White; small; in flat-topped clusters. *Fruit.* — Dark-purple.

The common elder borders the lanes and streams with its spreading flower-clusters in early summer, and in the later year is noticeable for the dark berries from which "elderberry wine" is brewed by the country people. The fine white wood is easily cut and is used for skewers and pegs. A decoction of the leaves serves the gardener a good purpose in protecting delicate plants from caterpillars. Evelyn* wrote of it: "If the medicinal properties of the leaves, berries, bark, etc., were thoroughly known, I cannot tell what our countrymen could ail for which he might not fetch from every hedge, whether from sickness or wound."

The white pith can easily be removed from the stems, hence the old English name of bore-wood.

The name elder is probably derived from the Anglo-Saxon *aeld* — a fire — and is thought to refer to the former use of the hollow branches in blowing up a fire.

WHITE FRINGED ORCHIS.

Habenaria blephariglottis. Orchid Family.

About one foot high. *Leaves.* — Oblong or lance-shaped; the upper passing into pointed bracts. *Flowers.* — Pure white; with a slender spur and fringed lip; growing in an oblong spike.

This seems to me the most exquisite of our native orchids. The fringed lips give the snowy, delicate flowers a feathery appearance as they gleam from the shadowy woods of midsummer, or from the peat-bogs where they thrive best; or perhaps they spire upward from among the dark green rushes which border some lonely

*John Evelyn, the English diarist (1620–1706).

mountain lake. Like the yellow fringed orchis, which they greatly resemble in general structure, they may be sought for in vain many seasons and then will be discovered, one midsummer day, lavishing their spotless loveliness upon some unsuspected marsh which has chanced to escape our vigilance.

LEAFY WHITE ORCHIS.

Habenaria dilatata. Orchid Family.

Stem. — Slender; leafy. *Leaves.* — Long and narrow. *Flowers.* — Small; white; with an incurved spur; growing in a slender spike.

The mention of the leafy white orchis recalls to my mind one midsummer morning in a New England swamp, where tangles of sheep laurel barred the way, branches of dogwood and azalea snapped into my eyes, while patches of fragrant adder's-mouth and fragile *Calopogon* just escaped being trodden underfoot, and exacted, by way of compensation, a breathless but delighted homage at their lovely shrines. Among tall-growing ferns, springing from elastic beds of moss, here I first found the slender, fragrant wands of this pretty orchid.

ROUND-LEAVED ORCHIS.

Habenaria orbiculata. Orchid Family.

Scape. — Stout, bracted, one to two feet high. *Basal leaves.* — Two, very large, orbicular, spreading flat on the ground, shining above, silvery beneath. *Flowers.* — Greenish-white, spreading in a loose raceme, with linear and slightly wedge-shaped lips and curved, slender spurs about an inch and a half long.

The peculiar charm of this orchid lies in its great flat rounded shining leaves, which spread themselves over the ground in an opulent fashion that seems to accord with the spirit of the deep pine woods where they are most at home. The tall scape with its many greenish-white flowers reaches maturity in July or August.

COMMON YARROW. MILFOIL.

Achillea millefolium. Composite Family.

Stem. — Simple at first, often branching near the summit. *Leaves.* — Divided into finely toothed segments. *Flower-heads.* — White, occasionally pink; clustered; small; made up of both ray and disk-flowers.

This is one of our most frequent roadside weeds, blossoming throughout the summer and late into the autumn. Tradition claims that it was used by Achilles to cure the wounds of his soldiers, and the genus is named after that mighty hero. It still forms one of the ingredients of an ointment valued by the Scotch Highlanders. The early English botanists called the plant "nose-bleed," "because the leaves being put into the nose caused it to bleed;" and Gerard writes that "Most men say that the leaves chewed, and especially greene, are a remedie for the toothache." These same pungent leaves also won it the name of "old man's pepper," while in Sweden its title signifies *field hop,* and refers to its employment in the manufacture of beer. Linnaeus considered the beer thus brewed to be more intoxicating than that in which hops were utilized. The old women of the Orkney Islands hold "milfoil tea" in high repute, believing it to be gifted with the power of dispelling melancholy. In

YARROW *Achillea millefolium*

Switzerland a good vinegar is said to be made from the Alpine species. The plant is cultivated in the gardens of Madeira, where so many beautiful and, in our eyes, rare, flowers grow in wild profusion.

WATER-HEMLOCK. SPOTTED COWBANE.

Cicuta maculata. Parsley Family.

Stem. — Smooth; stout; from two to six feet high; streaked with purple. *Leaves.* — Twice or thrice-compound; leaflets coarsely toothed. *Flowers.* — White; in compound umbels, the little umbels composed of numerous flowers.

This plant is often confused with the wild carrot, the sweet cicely, and other white-flowered members of the Parsley family; but usually it can be identified by its purple-streaked stem. The umbels of the water-hemlock are also more loosely clustered than those of the carrot, and their stalks are much more unequal. It is commonly found in marshy ground, blossoming in midsummer. Its popular names refer to its poisonous properties, its root being said to contain the most dangerous vegetable poison native to our country, and to have been frequently confounded with that of the edible sweet cicely with fatal results.

WATER-PARSNIP.

Sium suave. Parsley Family.

Two to six feet high. *Stem.* — Stout. *Leaves.* — Divided into from three to eight pairs of sharply toothed leaflets. *Flowers.* — White, in compound umbels.

This plant grows in water or wet places throughout North America. I have found it in great abundance both in swamps along the coast, and bordering mountain streams far inland. Its Parsley-like flower-clusters at once indicate the family of which it is a member.

SWEET CICELY.

Osmorhiza claytoni. Parsley Family.

One to three feet high. *Root.* — Thick; aromatic; edible. *Leaves.* — Twice or thrice-compound. *Flowers.* — White; small; growing in a somewhat flat-topped cluster.

This is one of the earliest-flowering of the white Parsleys. Its roots are prized by country children for their pleasant flavor. Great care should be taken not to confound this plant with the water-hemlock, which is very poisonous, and which it greatly resembles, although flowering earlier in the year. The generic name is from two Greek words which signify *scent* and *root.*

COW-PARSNIP.

Heracleum maximum. Parsley Family.

Stem. — Stout, often two inches thick at base, four to eight feet high, ridged, hollow, green. *Leaves.* — The lower large, compound in three divisions, leaflets lobed and sharply notched; on short leaf-stems which are much inflated and clasp the stalk; rank-smelling. *Flowers.* — In spreading, flat-topped clusters, white, with heart-shaped, notched petals; outer flowers larger than inner ones, and with irregular petals.

In swampy places this great vigorous looking plant, which blossoms in early summer, is often a conspicuous, and despite its coarseness, not altogether an unpleasing feature.

Purple-stemmed Angelica		Cow-Parsnip
Angelica atropurpurea		*Heracleum maximum*
(page 74)		(page 70)
	Boneset	
	Eupatorium perfoliatum	
	(page 81)	
Sweet Cicely		Common Yarrow
Osmorhiza claytoni		*Achillea millefolium*
(page 70)		(page 68)
	SUNNY CLUSTERS	

WILD CARROT. BIRD'S-NEST.
QUEEN ANNE'S LACE.

Daucus carota. Parsley Family.

Stems. — Tall and slender. *Leaves.* — Finely dissected. *Flowers.* — White; in a compound umbel, forming a circular flat-topped cluster.

When the delicate flowers of the wild carrot are still unsoiled by the dust from the highway, and fresh from the early summer rains, they are very beautiful, adding much to the appearance of the roadsides and fields along which they grow so abundantly as to strike despair into the heart of the farmer, for this is, perhaps, the "peskiest" of all the weeds with which he has to contend. As time goes on the blossoms begin to have a careworn look and lose something of the cobwebby aspect which won them the title of Queen Anne's lace. In late summer the flower-stalks erect themselves, forming a concave cluster which has the appearance of a bird's nest. I have read that a species of bee makes use of this ready-made home, but have never seen any indications of such an occupancy.

This is believed to be the stock from which the garden carrot

WILD CARROT *Daucus carota*

was raised. The vegetable was well known to the ancients, and we learn from Pliny that the finest specimens were brought to Rome from Candia. When it was first introduced into Great Britain is not known, although the supposition is that it was brought over by the Dutch during the reign of Elizabeth. In the writings of Parkinson* we read that the ladies wore carrot-leaves in their hair in place of feathers. One can picture the dejected appearance of a ball-room belle at the close of an entertainment.

PURPLE-STEMMED ANGELICA.

Angelica atropurpurea. Parsley Family.

Stem. — Stout, four to six feet high, smooth, dark purple. *Leaves.* — The lower very large, with inflated leaf-stems; compound in two or three divisions, these divided into lance-shaped or ovate sharply-toothed leaflets. *Flowers.* — White or greenish, in large spreading more or less flat-topped clusters.

In early summer, especially along the banks of streams and rivers, the great purple-stemmed angelica may be found spreading its flat-topped clusters of small greenish flowers. This plant may be distinguished from the cow-parsnip by its purple stem, and by its numerous pinnately-arranged leaflets.

WILD CUCUMBER.

Echinocystis lobata. Cucumber Family.

Stem. — Climbing; nearly smooth; with three-forked tendrils. *Leaves.* — Deeply and sharply five-lobed. *Flowers.* — Numerous; small; greenish-white; unisexual; the staminate ones growing in long racemes, the pistillate ones in small clusters or solitary. *Fruit.* — Fleshy; oval; green; about two inches long; clothed with weak prickles.

---

*John Parkinson, a seventeenth-century English botanist and herbalist.

This is an ornamental climber which is found bearing its flowers and fruit at the same time. It grows in rich soil along rivers in parts of New England, Pennsylvania, and westward; and is often culti-vated in gardens, making an effective arbor-vine. The generic name is from two Greek words which signify *hedgehog* and *bladder,* in reference to the prickly fruit.

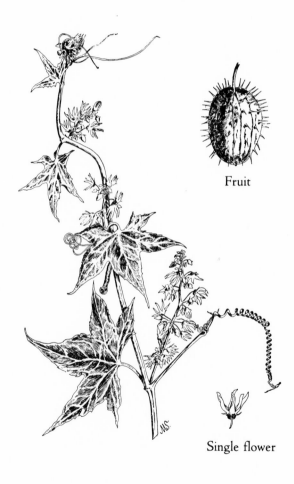

Fruit

Single flower

WILD CUCUMBER *Echinocystis lobata*

VIRGIN'S-BOWER. TRAVELLER'S-JOY.

Clematis virginiana. Buttercup Family.

Stem. — Climbing; somewhat woody. *Leaves.* — Opposite; three-divided. *Flowers.* — Whitish; in clusters; unisexual.

In July and August this beautiful plant, covered with its white blossoms and clambering over the shrubs which border the country lanes, makes indeed a fitting bower for any maid or traveller who may chance to be seeking shelter. Later in the year the seeds with their silvery plumes give a feathery effect, which is very striking.

This graceful climber works its way by means of its bending or clasping leaf-stalks. Darwin has made interesting experiments regarding the movements of the young shoots of the *Clematis*. He discovered that, "one revolved, describing a broad oval, in five hours, thirty minutes; and another in six hours, twelve minutes; they follow the course of the sun."

Fruit-cluster

VIRGIN'S-BOWER *Clematis virginiana*

COMMON DODDER. LOVE-VINE.

Cuscuta gronovii. Morning-glory Family.

Stems. — Yellow or reddish; thread-like; twining; leafless. *Flowers.* —
White; in close clusters.

Late in the summer perhaps we are tempted deep into some
thicket by the jasmine-scented heads of the buttonbush or the fragrant spikes of the *Clethra,* and note for the first time the tangled
golden threads and close white flower-clusters of the dodder. If we
try to trace to their source these twisted stems, which the Creoles
know as "angels' hair," we discover that they are fastened to the
bark of the shrub or plant about which they are twining by means
of small suckers; but nowhere can we find any connection with the
earth, all their nourishment being extracted from the plant to which
they are adhering. Originally this curious herb sprang from the
ground which succored it until it succeeded in attaching itself to
some plant; having accomplished this it severed all connection with
mother-earth by the withering away or snapping off of the stem
below.

The flax-dodder, *C. epilinum,* is a very injurious plant in European flax-fields. It has been sparingly introduced into this country
with flax-seed.

GROUND-CHERRY.

Physalis virginiana. Tomato Family.

A strong-scented, low, much-branched and spreading herb. *Leaves.* —
Somewhat oblong or heart-shaped; wavy-toothed. *Flowers.* — Greenish
or yellowish-white; solitary on nodding flower-stalks. *Fruit.* — A green
or yellow edible berry.

We find the ground-cherry in light sandy soil, and are more apt
to notice the loosely enveloped berry of the late year than the
rather inconspicuous flowers which appear in summer.

TURTLEHEAD.

Chelone glabra. Snapdragon Family.

One to seven feet high. *Stem.* — Smooth; upright; branching. *Leaves.* — Opposite; lance-shaped; toothed. *Flowers.* — White or pinkish; growing in a spike or close cluster.

TURTLEHEAD *Chelone glabra*

It seems to have been my fate to find the flowers which the botany relegates to "dry, sandy soil" flourishing luxuriantly in marshes; and to encounter the flowers which by right belong to "wet woods" flaunting themselves in sunny meadows. This cannot be attributed to the natural depravity of inanimate objects, for what is more full of life than the flowers? — and no one would believe in their depravity except perhaps the amateur-botanist who is endeavoring to master the different species of goldenrods and asters. Therefore it is pleasant to record that I do not remember ever having met a turtlehead, which is assigned by the botany to "wet places," which had not gotten as close to a stream or a marsh or a moist ditch as it well could without actually wetting its feet. The flowers of this plant are more odd and striking than pretty. Their appearance is such that their common name seems fairly appropriate. I have heard unbotanical people call them "white closed gentians."

CLIMBING FALSE BUCKWHEAT.

Polygonum scandens. Buckwheat Family.

Stem. — Smooth; twining, and climbing over bushes; eight to twelve feet high. *Leaves.* — Heart or arrow shaped; pointed; alternate. *Flowers.* — Greenish or pinkish; in racemes. *Seed-vessel.* — Green; three-angled; winged; conspicuous in autumn.

In early summer this plant, which clambers so perseveringly over the moist thickets which line our country lanes, is comparatively inconspicuous. The racemes of small greenish flowers are not likely to attract one's attention, and it is late summer or autumn before the thick clusters of greenish fruit, composed of the winged seed-vessels, arrest one's notice. At this time the vine is very beautiful and striking, and one wonders that it could have escaped detection in the earlier year.

WHITE SNAKEROOT.

Eupatorium rugosum. Composite Family.

About three feet high. *Stem.* — Smooth and branching. *Leaves.* —
Opposite; long-stalked; broadly ovate; coarsely and sharply toothed.
Flower-heads. — White; clustered; composed of tubular blossoms.

This species is less common but more beautiful and effective
than the boneset. It is found blossoming in the rich northern woods
of late summer.

WHITE SNAKEROOT *Eupatorium rugosum*

BONESET. THOROUGHWORT.

Eupatorium perfoliatum. Composite Family.

Stem. — Stout and hairy; two to four feet high. *Leaves.* — Opposite; widely spreading; lance-shaped; united at the base around the stem. *Flower-heads.* — Dull white; small; composed entirely of tubular blossoms borne in large clusters.

To one whose childhood was passed in the country some fifty years ago the name or sight of this plant is fraught with unpleasant memories. The attic or wood-shed was hung with bunches of the

BONESET *Eupatorium perfoliatum*

dried herb, which served as so many grewsome warnings against wet feet, or any over-exposure which might result in cold or malaria. A certain Nemesis, in the shape of a nauseous draught which was poured down the throat under the name of "boneset tea," attended such a catastrophe. The Indians first discovered its virtues, and named the plant ague-weed. Possibly this is one of the few herbs whose efficacy has not been overrated. Dr. Millspaugh* says: "It is prominently adapted to cure a disease peculiar to the South, known as break-bone fever (Dengue), and it is without doubt from this property that the name boneset was derived."

---

*Charles Frederick Millspaugh (1854–1923), a renowned botanist and physician who taught at the University of Chicago.

False Solomon's-Seal
Smilacina racemosa
(page 24)

Mountain Laurel
Kalmia latifolia
(page 34)

Selfheal
Prunella vulgaris
(page 246)

Sheep Laurel
Kalmia augustifolia
(page 176)

Ginseng
Panax quinquefolius
(page 18)

Herb-Robert
Geranium robertianum
(page 186)

Pipsissewa
Chimaphila umbellata
(page 45)

Indian-Pipe
Monotropa uniflora
(page 46)

One-Flowered Wintergreen
Moneses uniflora
(page 33)

Partridgeberry
Mitchella repens
(page 54)

SUMMER SHADE

TALL MEADOW-RUE.

Thalictrum polygamum. Buttercup Family.

Four to eight feet high. *Leaves.* — Divided into many firm, rounded leaflets. *Flowers.* — White; in large clusters; some perfect, others unisexual.

When a stream trails its sluggish length through the fields of midsummer, its way is oftentimes marked by the tall meadow-rue, the feathery, graceful flower-clusters of which erect themselves serenely above the myriad blossoms which are making radiant the wet meadows at this season. For, here, too, we may search for the

TALL MEADOW-RUE *Thalictrum polygamum*

purple flag and fringed orchis, the Canada lily, the pink swamp-milkweed, each charming in its way, but none with the cool chaste beauty of the meadow-rue. The staminate flowers of this plant are especially delicate and feathery.

BROAD-LEAVED ARROWHEAD.

Sagittaria latifolia. Arrowhead Family.

Scape. — A few inches to several feet high. *Leaves.* — Arrow-shaped. *Flowers.* — White; unisexual; in whorls of three on the leafless scape.

Among our water-flowers none are more delicately lovely than those of the arrowhead. Fortunately the ugly and inconspicuous female flowers grow on the lower whorls, while the male ones, with their snowy petals and golden centres, are arranged about the upper part of the scape, where the eye first falls. It is a pleasure to chance upon a slow stream whose margins are bordered with these fragile blossoms and bright, arrow-shaped leaves.

LADIES'-TRESSES.

Spiranthes cernua. Orchid Family.

Stem. — Leafy below, leafy-bracted above; six to twenty inches high. *Leaves.* — Linear-lance-shaped; the lowest elongated. *Flowers.* — White; fragrant; the lips wavy or crisped; growing in slender spikes.

This pretty little orchid is found in great abundance in September and October. The botany relegates it to "wet places," but I have seen dry upland pastures as well as low-lying swamps profusely flecked with its slender, fragrant spikes. The braided appearance of these spikes would easily account for the popular name of ladies'-tresses; but we learn that the plant's English name was formerly "ladies' *traces*," from a fancied resemblance between its

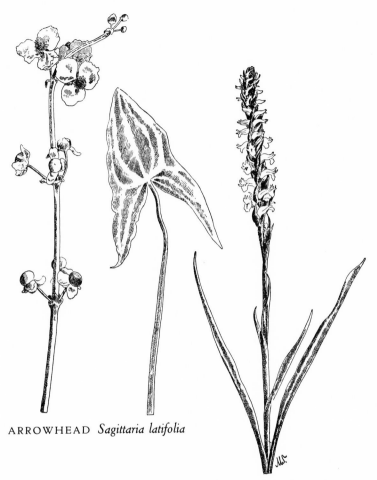

ARROWHEAD *Sagittaria latifolia*

LADIES'-TRESSES *Spiranthes cernua*

twisted clusters and the lacings which played so important a part in the feminine toilet. I am told that in parts of New England the country people have christened the plant "wild hyacinth."

The flowers of *S. gracilis* are very small, and grow in a much more slender, one-sided spike than those of *S. cernua*. They are found in the dry woods and along the sandy hill-sides from July onward.

FRAGRANT WATER-LILY.

Nymphaea odorata. Water-lily Family.

Leaves. — Rounded; somewhat heart-shaped; floating on the surface of the water. *Flowers.* — Large; white or sometimes pink; fragrant.

This exquisite flower calls for little description. Many of us are so fortunate as to hold in our memories golden mornings devoted to its quest. We can hardly take the shortest railway journey in summer without passing some shadowy pool whose greatest adornment is this spotless and queenly blossom. The breath of the lily-pond is brought even into the heart of our cities, where children peddle clusters of the long-stemmed fragrant flowers about the streets.

In the water-lily may be seen an example of so-called *plant-metamorphosis.* The petals appear to pass gradually into stamens, it being difficult to decide where the petals end and the stamens begin. But whether stamens are transformed petals, or petals transformed stamens, seems to be a mooted question. In Gray* we read, "Petals numerous, in many series, the innermost gradually passing into stamens;" while Mr. Grant Allen** writes: "Petals are in all probability enlarged and flattened stamens, which have been set apart for the work of attracting insects," and goes on to say, "Flowers can and do exist without petals, ... but no flower can possibly exist without stamens, which are one of the two essential reproductive organs in the plant." From this he argues that it is more rational to consider a petal a transformed stamen than *vice versa.* To go further into the subject here would be impossible, but a careful study of the water-lily is likely to excite one's curiosity in the matter.

---

*Asa Gray, the eminent botanist and writer whose *Manual of Botany,* compiled in the mid-nineteenth century, is still a standard American reference.
**An English writer, scientist, and philosopher (1848–1899).

II

YELLOW

MARSH-MARIGOLD *Caltha palustris*

MARSH-MARIGOLD. COWSLIP.

Caltha palustris. Buttercup Family.

Stem. — Hollow; furrowed. *Leaves.* — Rounded; somewhat kidney-shaped. *Flowers.* — Golden-yellow.

> "Hark, hark! the lark at heaven's gate sings,
>   And Phœbus 'gins arise,
> His steeds to water at those springs
>   On chalic'd flowers that lies;
> And winking Mary-buds begin
>   To ope their golden eyes;
> With everything that pretty is —
>   My lady sweet, arise!
>   Arise, arise." — *Cymbeline.*

We claim — and not without authority — that these "winking Mary-buds" are identical with the gay marsh-marigolds which border our springs and gladden our wet meadows every April. There are those who assert that the poet had in mind the garden marigold — *Calendula* — but surely no cultivated flower could harmonize with the spirit of the song as do these gleaming swamp blossoms. We will yield to the garden if necessary —

> "The marigold that goes to bed with the sun
> And with him rises weeping —"

of the "Winter's Tale," but insist on retaining for that larger, lovelier garden in which we all feel a certain sense of possession — even if we are not taxed on real estate in any part of the country — the "golden eyes" of the Mary-bud; and we feel strengthened in our position by the statement in Mr. Robinson's "Wild Garden"* that the marsh-marigold is so abundant along certain English rivers as to cause the ground to look as though paved with gold at those seasons when they overflow their banks.

These flowers are peddled about our streets every spring under the name of cowslips — a title to which they have no claim, and

---

*William Robinson, the British landscape designer (1838–1935).

which is the result of that reckless fashion of christening unrecognized flowers which is so prevalent, and which is responsible for so much confusion about their English names.

The plant is a favorite "pot-herb" with country people, far superior, I am told, to spinach; the young flower-buds also are considered palatable.

The derivation of marigold is somewhat obscure. In the "Grete Herball" of the sixteenth century the flower is spoken of as *Mary Gowles,* and by the early English poets as *gold* simply. As the first part of the word might be derived from the Anglo-Saxon *mere* — a marsh, it seems possible that the entire name may signify *marshgold,* which would be an appropriate and poetic title for this shining flower of the marshes.

YELLOW ADDER'S-TONGUE.
DOG'S-TOOTH-VIOLET.

Erythronium americanum. Lily Family.

Scape. — Six to nine inches high; one-flowered. *Leaves.* — Two; oblong-lance-shaped; pale green mottled with purple and white. *Flowers.* — Rather large; pale yellow marked with purple; nodding.

The white blossoms of the shadbush gleam from the thicket, and the sheltered hill-side is already starred with the bloodroot and anemone when we go to seek the yellow adder's-tongue. We direct our steps toward one of those hollows in the wood which is watered by such a clear gurgling brook as must appeal to every country-loving heart; and there where the pale April sunlight filters through the leafless branches, nod myriads of these lilies, each one guarded by a pair of mottled, erect, sentinel-like leaves.

The two English names of this plant are unsatisfactory and inappropriate. If the marking of its leaves resembles the skin of an adder why name it after its tongue? And there is equally little reason for calling a lily a violet. Mr. Burroughs* has suggested two

---

*John Burroughs, the American naturalist and author (1837–1921).

pretty and significant names. "Fawn lily," he thinks, would be appropriate, because a fawn is also mottled, and because the two leaves stand up with the alert, startled look of a fawn's ears. The speckled foliage and perhaps its flowering season are indicated in the title "trout-lily," which has a spring-like flavor not without charm. It is said that the early settlers of Pennsylvania named the flower "yellow snowdrop," in memory of their own "harbinger-of-spring."

The white dog's-tooth-violet, *E. albidum,* is a species which is usually found somewhat westward.

Bulb

YELLOW ADDER'S-TONGUE *Erythronium americanum*

WILD OATS.

Uvularia sessilifolia. Lily Family.

Stem. — Acutely angled; rather low. *Leaves.* — Set close to or clasping the stem; pale; lance-oblong. *Flower.* — Yellowish or straw-color.

In spring this little plant is very abundant in the woods. It bears one or two small lily-like blossoms which droop modestly beneath the curving stems.

Near of kin is Bellwort, *U. perfoliata,* with leaves which seem pierced by the stem, but otherwise of a strikingly similar aspect.

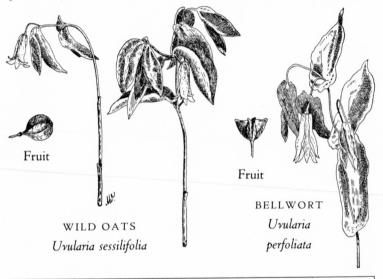

Fruit

Fruit

WILD OATS
Uvularia sessilifolia

BELLWORT
*Uvularia
perfoliata*

Cardinal-Flower
Lobelia cardinalis
(page 223)

Pickerelweed
Pontederia cordata
(page 245)

Grass-of-Parnassus
Parnassia glauca
(page 40)

Wild Calla
Calla palustris
(page 28)

Marsh-Marigold
Caltha palustris
(page 91)

WATER'S EDGE

SOLOMON'S-SEAL.

Polygonatum biflorum. Lily Family.

Stem. — Slender; curving; one to three feet long. *Leaves.* — Alternate; oval; set close to the stem. *Flowers.* — Yellowish; bell-shaped; nodding from the axils of the leaves. *Fruit.* — A dark blue berry.

The graceful leafy stems of the Solomon's-seal are among the most decorative features of our spring woods. The small blossoms which appear in May grow either singly or in clusters on a flower-stalk which is so fastened into the axil of each leaf that they droop beneath, forming a curve of singular grace which is sustained in later summer by the dark blue berries.

The larger species, *P. canaliculatum,* grows to a height of from two to seven feet, blossoming in the meadows and along the streams in June.

The common name was suggested by the rootstocks, which are marked with large round scars left by the death and separation of the base of the stout stalks of the previous years. These scars somewhat resemble the impression of a seal upon wax.

The generic name is from two Greek words signifying *many* and *knee,* alluding to the numerous joints of the rootstock.

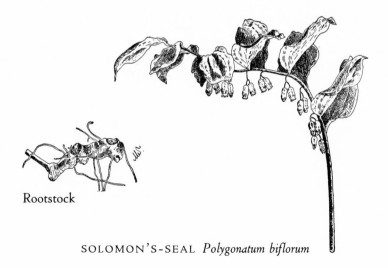

Rootstock

SOLOMON'S-SEAL *Polygonatum biflorum*

CELANDINE-POPPY.

Stylophorum diphyllum. Poppy Family.

Stem. — Low; two-leaved. *Stem-leaves.* — Opposite; deeply incised. *Root-leaves.* — Incised or divided. *Flowers.* — Deep-yellow; large; one or more at the summit of the stem.

In April or May, somewhat south and westward, the woods are brightened, and occasionally the hill-sides are painted yellow, by this handsome flower. In both flower and foliage the plant suggests the celandine.

CELANDINE.

Chelidonium majus. Poppy Family.

Stem. — Brittle; with saffron-colored, acrid juice. *Leaves.* — Compound or divided; toothed or cut. *Flowers.* — Yellow; clustered. *Pod.* — Slender; linear.

The name of celandine must always suggest the poet who never seemed to weary of writing in its honor:

> "Pansies, lilies, kingcups, daisies,
> Let them live upon their praises;
> Long as there's a sun that sets,
> Primroses will have their glory;
> Long as there are violets,
> They will have a place in story;
> There's a flower that shall be mine,
> 'Tis the little celandine."

And when certain yellow flowers which frequent the village roadside are pointed out to us as those of the celandine, we feel a sense of disappointment that the favorite theme of Wordsworth should arouse within us so little enthusiasm. So perhaps we are rather relieved than otherwise to realize that the botanical name of this plant signifies *greater* celandine; for we remember that the poet never failed to specify the *small* celandine as the object of his praise. The small [lesser] celandine is *Ranunculus ficaria,* one of the Buttercup family, and is only found in this country as an escape from gardens.

CELANDINE
Chelidonium majus

GOLDEN CLUB.

Orontium aquaticum. Arum Family.

Scape. — Slender; elongated. *Leaves.* — Long-stalked; oblong; floating. *Flowers.* — Small; yellow; crowded over the narrow spike or spadix.

When we go to the bogs in May to hunt for the purple flower of the pitcher-plant we are likely to chance upon the well-named golden club. This curious-looking club-shaped object, which is found along the borders of ponds, indicates its relationship to the Jack-in-the-Pulpit, and still more to the calla-lily, but unlike them its tiny flowers are shielded by no protecting spathe.

Kalm tells us in his "Travels," "that the Indians called the plant *Taw-Kee,* and used its dried seeds as food."

DOWNY YELLOW VIOLET.

Viola pubescens. Violet Family.

Stems. — Leafy above; erect. *Leaves.* — Broadly heart-shaped; toothed. *Flowers.* — Yellow, veined with purple; otherwise much like those of the common blue violet.

"When beechen buds begin to swell,
    And woods the blue-bird's warble know,
The yellow violet's modest bell
    Peeps from the last year's leaves below,"

sings Bryant, in his charming, but not strictly accurate poem, for the chances are that the "beechen buds" have almost burst into foliage, and that the "blue-bird's warble" has been heard for some time when these pretty flowers begin to dot the woods.

WINTER CRESS. YELLOW ROCKET.

Barbarea vulgaris. Mustard Family.

Stem. — Smooth. *Leaves.* — The lower lyre-shaped; the upper ovate, toothed or deeply incised at their base. *Flowers.* — Yellow; growing in racemes. *Pod.* — Linear; erect or slightly spreading.

As early as May we find the bright flowers of the winter cress along the roadside. This is probably the first of the yellow mustards to appear.

DOWNY YELLOW VIOLET
Viola pubescens

WINTER CRESS *Barbarea vulgaris*

DANDELION.

Taraxacum officinale. Composite Family.

If Emerson's definition of a weed, as a plant whose virtues have not yet been discovered, be correct, we can hardly place the dandelion in that category, for its young sprouts have been valued as a pot-herb, its fresh leaves enjoyed as a salad, and its dried roots used as a substitute for coffee in various countries and ages. It is said that the Apache Indians so greatly relished it as food, that they scoured the country for many days in order to procure enough to appease their appetites, and that the quantity consumed by one individual exceeded belief. The feathery-tufted seeds which form the downy balls beloved as "clocks" by country children, are delicately and beautifully adapted to dissemination by the wind, which ingenious arrangement partly accounts for the plant's wide range. The common name is a corruption of the French *dent de lion*. There is a difference of opinion as to which part of the plant is supposed to resemble a lion's tooth. Some fancy the jagged leaves gave rise to the name, while others claim that it refers to the yellow flowers, which they liken to the golden teeth of the heraldic lion. In nearly every European country the plant bears a name of similar significance.

Purple-flowering Raspberry
Rubus odoratus
(page 136)

Blue Vervain
Verbena hastata
(page 242)

Ragged Fringed Orchis
Habenaria lacera
(page 148)

American Brooklime
Veronica americana
(page 236)

Shinleaf
Pyrola elliptica
(page 39)

Wild Pink
Silene caroliniana
var. *pensylvanica*
(page 160)

Carrion-Flower
Smilax herbacea
(page 272)

Dewdrop
Dalibarda repens
(page 49)

Twinflower
Linnaea borealis
(page 155)

Wood-Sorrel
Oxalis montana
(page 37)

MIDSUMMER

WHORLED LOOSESTRIFE.

Lysimachia quadrifolia. Primrose Family.

Stem. — Slender; one to two feet high. *Leaves.* — Narrowly oblong; whorled in fours, fives, or sixes. *Flowers.* — Yellow, spotted or streaked with red; on slender, hair-like flower-stalks from the axils of the leaves.

This slender pretty plant grows along the roadsides and attracts one's notice in June by its regular whorls of leaves and flowers. Linnaeus says that this genus is named after Lysimachus, King of Sicily. Loosestrife is the English for Lysimachus; but whether the ancient superstition that the placing of these flowers upon the yokes of oxen rendered the beasts gentle and submissive arose from the peace-suggestive title or from other causes, I cannot discover.

WHORLED LOOSESTRIFE *Lysimachia quadrifolia*

YELLOW LOOSESTRIFE. SWAMP-CANDLES.

Lysimachia terrestris. Primrose Family.

Stem. — One to two feet high; leafy. *Leaves.* — Opposite; lance-shaped. *Flowers.* — Small; yellow; growing in long clusters.

The bright clusters of the yellow loosestrife shoot upward from the marshes, and gild the brook's border from June till August.

YELLOW LOOSESTRIFE *Lysimachia terrestris*

FRINGED LOOSESTRIFE
Lysimachia ciliata

FRINGED LOOSESTRIFE.

Lysimachia ciliata. Primrose Family.

Stem. — Erect; two to four feet high. *Leaves.* — Opposite; narrowly oval; on fringed leaf-stalks. *Flowers.* — Yellow; on slender stalks from the axils of the leaves.

This plant is nearly akin to the swamp-candles. It abounds in low grounds and thickets, putting forth its bright wheel-shaped blossoms early in July.

YELLOW LADY'S-SLIPPER.
WHIP-POOR-WILL SHOE.

Cypripedium calceolus. Orchid Family.

Stem. — About two feet high; downy; leafy to the top; one to three-flowered. *Leaves.* — Alternate; broadly oval; many-nerved and plaited. *Flower.* — Large; the pale yellow lip an inflated pouch; the two lateral petals long and narrow; wavy-twisted; brownish.

The yellow lady's-slipper usually blossoms in May or June, a few days later than its pink sister, *C. acaule.* Regarding its favorite haunts, Mr. Baldwin* says: "Its preference is for maples, beeches, and particularly butternuts, and for sloping or hilly ground, and I always look with glad suspicion at a knoll covered with ferns, cohoshes, and trilliums, expecting to see a clump of this plant among them. Its sentinel-like habit of choosing 'sightly places' leads it to venture well up on mountain sides."

The long, wavy, brownish petals give the flower an alert, startled look when surprised in its lonely hiding-places.

The small yellow lady's-slipper, another variety of *C. calceolus,* is richer in color though smaller in size. It has also the charm of fragrance.

INDIAN CUCUMBER-ROOT.

Medeola virginiana. Lily Family.

Root. — Tuberous; shaped somewhat like a cucumber, with a suggestion of its flavor. *Stem.* — Slender; from one to three feet high; at first clothed with wool. *Leaves.* — In two whorls on the flowering plants; the lower of five to nine oblong, pointed leaves set close to the stem; the upper usually of three or four much smaller ones. *Flowers.* — Greenish-yellow; small; clustered; recurved; set close to the upper leaves. *Fruit.* — A purple berry.

One is more apt to pause in September to note the brilliant foliage and purple berries of this little plant than to gather the

---

Orchids of New England. William Baldwin (1779–1819) was a physician as well as a botanist.

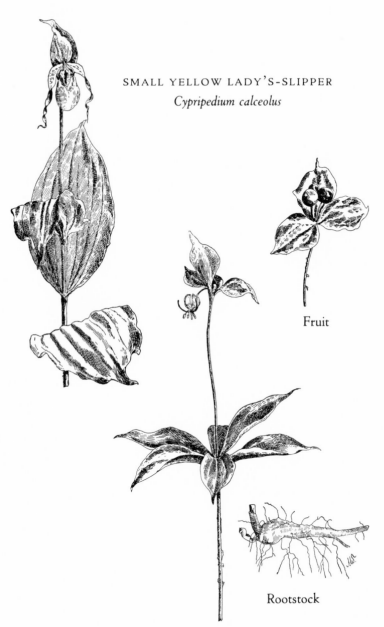

SMALL YELLOW LADY'S-SLIPPER
Cypripedium calceolus

Fruit

Rootstock

INDIAN CUCUMBER-ROOT
Medeola virginiana

drooping inconspicuous blossoms for his bunch of wood-flowers in June. The generic name is after the sorceress Medea, on account of its supposed medicinal virtues, of which, however, there seems to be no record.

The tuberous rootstock has the flavor, and something the shape, of the cucumber, and was probably used as food by the Indians. It would not be an uninteresting study to discover which of our common wild plants are able to afford pleasant and nutritious food; in such a pursuit many of the otherwise unattractive popular names would prove suggestive.

SILVERY CINQUEFOIL.

Potentilla argentea. Rose Family.

Stems. — Ascending; branched at the summit; white; woolly. *Leaves.* — Divided into five wedge-oblong, deeply incised leaflets, which are green above, white with silvery wool beneath. *Flowers.* — Much as in above.

The silvery cinquefoil has rather large yellow flowers, which are found in dry fields throughout the summer as far south as New Jersey.

		Pokeweed
Tansy		*Phytolacca americana*
Tanacetum vulgare	Elecampane	(page 58)
(page 147)	*Inula helenium*	
	(page 128)	
Viper's Bugloss		Shrubby Cinquefoil
Echium vulgare	Prickly Pear	*Potentilla fruticosa*
(page 248)	*Opuntia humifusa*	(page 113)
	(page 121)	
	LATE SUMMER	

SHRUBBY CINQUEFOIL. FIVE-FINGER.

Potentilla fruticosa. Rose Family.

Stem. — Erect; shrubby; one to four feet high. *Leaves.* — Divided into five to seven narrow leaflets. *Flowers.* — Yellow; resembling those of the common cinquefoil, but larger.

Of all the cinquefoils perhaps this one most truly merits the title five-finger. Certainly its slender leaflets are much more finger-like than those of the common cinquefoil. It is not a common plant in most localities, but is very abundant among the Berkshire Hills, where it takes entire possession of otherwise barren fields and roadsides; its peculiarly bluish-green foliage and bright yellow flowers (looking like buttercups growing on a shrub) arresting one's attention throughout the entire summer and occasionally late into the autumn.

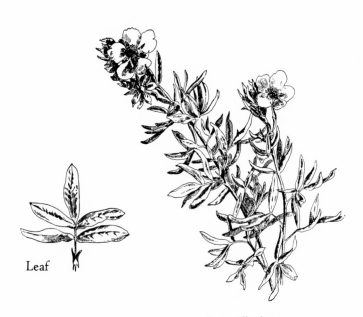

Leaf

SHRUBBY CINQUEFOIL *Potentilla fruticosa*

COMMON CINQUEFOIL. FIVE-FINGER.

Potentilla canadensis. Rose Family.

Stem. — Slender; prostrate, or sometimes erect. *Leaves.* — Divided really into three leaflets, but apparently into five by the parting of the lateral leaflets. *Flowers.* — Yellow; growing singly from the axils of the leaves.

From spring to nearly midsummer the roads are bordered and the fields carpeted with the bright flowers of the common cinquefoil. The passer-by unconsciously betrays his recognition of some of the prominent features of the Rose family by often assuming that the plant is a yellow-flowered wild strawberry. Both of the English names refer to the pretty foliage, cinquefoil being derived from the French *cinq feuilles.* The generic name, *Potentilla,* has reference to the powerful medicinal properties formerly attributed to the genus.

ROUGH CINQUEFOIL.

Potentilla norvegica. Rose Family.

Stout, rough, six inches to two and one-half feet high, with many leafy bracts. *Leaves.* — Divided into three obovate leaflets. *Flowers.* — Yellow, in rather close, leafy clusters.

This rather weedy-looking plant is often common in dry soil, flowering throughout the summer.

HOP CLOVER. YELLOW CLOVER.

Trifolium agrarium. Pea Family.

Six to twelve inches high. *Leaves.* — Divided into three oblong leaflets. *Flowers.* — Yellow; small; in close heads.

Although this little plant is found in such abundance along our New England roadsides and in many other parts of the country as well, comparatively few people seem to recognize it as a member of the clover group, despite a marked likeness in the leaves and blossoms to others of the same family.

The name clover probably originated in the Latin *clava* (clubs), in reference to the fancied resemblance between the three-pronged club of Hercules and the clover leaf. The clubs of our playing-cards and the *trèfle* (trefoil) of the French are probably an imitation of the same leaf.

The nonesuch, *Medicago lupulina,* with downy, procumbent stems, and flowers which grow in short spikes, is nearly allied to the hop clover. In its reputed superiority as fodder its English name is said to have originated. Dr. Prior says that for many years this plant has been recognized in Ireland as the true shamrock.

HOP CLOVER
Trifolium agrarium

COMMON ST. JOHNSWORT.

Hypericum perforatum. St. Johnswort Family.

Stem. — Much branched. *Leaves.* — Small; opposite; somewhat oblong; with pellucid dots. *Flowers.* — Yellow; numerous; in leafy clusters.

"Too well known as a pernicious weed which it is difficult to extirpate," is the scornful notice which the botany gives to this plant, whose bright yellow flowers are noticeable in waste fields and along roadsides nearly all summer. Its rank, rapid growth proves very exhausting to the soil, and every New England farmer wishes it had remained where it rightfully belongs — on the other side of the water.

Perhaps more superstitions have clustered about the St. Johnswort than about any other plant on record. It was formerly gathered on St. John's eve, and was hung at the doors and windows as a safeguard against thunder and evil spirits. A belief prevailed that on this night the soul had power to leave the body and visit the spot where it would finally be summoned from its earthly habitation, hence the all-night vigils which were observed at that time.

"The wonderful herb whose leaf will decide
If the coming year shall make me a bride,"

is the St. Johnswort, and the maiden's fate is favorably forecast by the healthy growth and successful blossoming of the plant which she has accepted as typical of her future.

In early times poets and physicians alike extolled its properties. An ointment was made of its blossoms, and one of its early names was "balm-of-the-warrior's-wound." It was considered so efficacious a remedy for melancholia that it was termed "fuga daemonum." Very possibly this name gave rise to the general idea that it was powerful in dispelling evil spirits.

The pale St. Johnswort, *H. ellipticum,* has thin, spreading, oval leaves which are set close to the stem, and pale yellow flowers, about half an inch broad.

The spotted St. Johnswort, *H. punctatum,* may be identified by its slender blossoms and copiously black-dotted, oblong leaves.

The Canadian St. Johnswort, *H. canadense,* has linear three-nerved leaves and small flowers with from five to twelve stamens only. It grows abundantly in wet, sandy places.

The dwarf St. Johnswort, *H. mutilum,* has even smaller blossoms, with from five to twelve stamens also, and narrowly oblong or ovate leaves, which are five-nerved and partly clasping. This is abundant in low grounds everywhere.

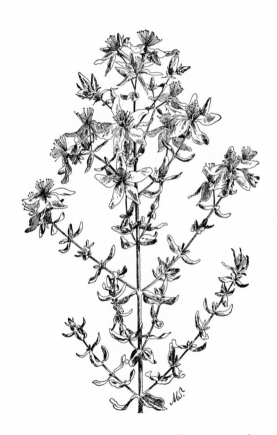

COMMON ST. JOHNSWORT *Hypericum perforatum*

YELLOW STARGRASS.

Hypoxis hirsuta. Daffodil Family.

Scapes. — Slender; few-flowered. *Leaves.* — Linear; grass-like; hairy. *Flowers.* — Yellow.

When our eyes fall upon what looks like a bit of evening sky set with golden stars, but which proves to be only a piece of shaded turf gleaming with these pretty flowers, we recall Longfellow's musical lines:

> "Spake full well in language quaint and olden,
> One who dwelleth on the castled Rhine,
> When he called the flowers so blue and golden,
> Stars, which in earth's firmament do shine."

The plant grows abundantly in open woods and meadows flowering in early summer.

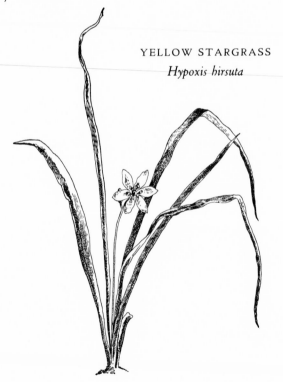

YELLOW STARGRASS
Hypoxis hirsuta

RATTLESNAKE-WEED.

Hieracium venosum. Composite Family.

Stem or Scape. — One to two feet high; naked or with a single leaf; slender; forking above. *Leaves.* — From the root; oblong; often making a sort of flat rosette; usually conspicuously veined with purple. *Flower-heads.* — Yellow; composed entirely of strap-shaped flowers.

The loosely clustered yellow flower-heads of the rattlesnake-weed somewhat resemble small dandelions. They abound in the pine-woods and dry, waste places of early summer. The purple-veined leaves, whose curious markings give to the plant its common name, grow close to the ground and are supposed to be efficacious

RATTLESNAKE-WEED

Hieracium venosum

in rattlesnake bites. Here again crops out the old "doctrine of signatures," for undoubtedly this virtue has been attributed to the species solely on account of the fancied resemblance between its leaves and the markings of the rattlesnake.

Another yellow species which is found in the dry open woods is the rough hawkweed, *H. scabrum*. This plant may be distinguished from the rattlesnake-weed not only by its unveined leaves, but by its *leafy*, rough, rather stout stem. Its thick flower-stalks, and the involucre which surrounds each flower-head, are densely clothed with dark hairs.

The panicled hawkweed, *H. paniculatum*, found also in dry woods, is usually smooth throughout. Its leafy stem is branched above, with slender, often drooping flower-stalks.

CANADA LILY. WILD YELLOW LILY.

Lilium canadense. Lily Family.

Stem. — Two to five feet high. *Leaves.* — Whorled; lance-shaped. *Flowers.* — Yellow, spotted with reddish-brown; bell-shaped; two to three inches long.

What does the summer bring which is more enchanting than a sequestered wood-bordered meadow hung with a thousand of these delicate, nodding bells which look as though ready to tinkle at the least disturbance and sound an alarm among the flowers?

These too are true "lilies of the field," less gorgeous, less imposing than the Turk's-caps, but with an unsurpassed grace and charm of their own. "Fairy-caps" these pointed blossoms are sometimes called; "witch-caps" would be more appropriate still. Indeed they would make dainty headgear for any of the dim inhabitants of Wonder-land.

The growth of this plant is very striking when seen at its best. The erect stem is surrounded with regular whorls of leaves, from the upper one of which curves a circle of long-stemmed, nodding flowers. They suggest an exquisite design for church candelabra.

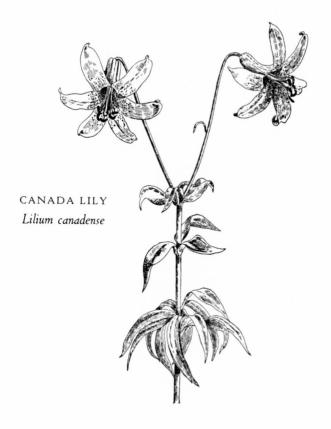

CANADA LILY
Lilium canadense

PRICKLY PEAR. INDIAN FIG.

Opuntia humifusa. Cactus Family.

Flowers. — Yellow; large; two and a half to three and a half inches across. *Fruit.* — Shaped like a small pear; often with prickles over its surface.

This curious looking plant is the only representative of the Cactus family in the Northeastern States. It has deep green, fleshy, prickly, rounded joints and large yellow flowers, which are often conspicuous in summer in dry, sandy places along the coast. Another form of *O. humifusa* has somewhat smaller flowers.

SPATTERDOCK. YELLOW POND-LILY.

Nuphar advena. Water-lily Family.

Leaves. — Floating or erect; roundish to oblong; with a deep cleft at their base. *Flowers.* — Yellow; sometimes purplish; large; somewhat globular.

Bordering the slow streams and stagnant ponds from May till August may be seen the yellow pond-lilies. These flowers lack the delicate beauty and fragrance of the white water-lilies; having, indeed, either from their odor, or appearance, or the form of their fruit, won for themselves in England the unpoetic title of "brandy-bottle." Owing to their love of mud they have also been called "frog-lilies." The Indians used their roots for food.

SUNDROPS.

Oenothera fruticosa. Evening-primrose Family.

Stem. — Erect; one to three feet high. *Leaves.* — Alternate; oblong to narrowly lance-shaped. *Flowers.* — Bright yellow; rather large; usually somewhat loosely clustered.

This is a day-blooming species of the evening-primrose. Its pretty delicate flowers abound along the roadsides and in the meadows of early summer.

O. perennis is another day-bloomer belonging to this same genus. Its flowers are much smaller than the sundrops'.

Broad-leaved Arrowhead
Sagittaria latifolia
(page 86)

Golden Club
Orontium aquaticum
(page 99)

Water-Stargrass
Heteranthera dubia

Watercress
Nasturtium officinale
(page 12)

Spatterdock
Nuphar advena
(page 122)

Fragrant Water-Lily
Nymphaea odorata
(page 88)

POND AND STREAM

BLACK-EYED SUSAN. CONEFLOWER.

Rudbeckia hirta. Composite Family.

Stem. — Stout and hairy; one to two feet high. *Leaves.* — Rough and hairy. *Flower-heads.* — Composed of both ray and disk-flowers; the former yellow, the latter brown and arranged on a cone-like receptacle.

By the middle of July our dry meadows are merry with black-eyed Susans, which are laughing from every corner and keeping up a gay midsummer carnival in company with the yellow lilies and brilliant milkweeds. They seem to revel in the long days of blazing sunlight, and are veritable salamanders among the flowers. Although now so common in our eastern fields they were first brought to us with clover-seed from the west, and are not altogether acceptable guests, as they bid fair to add another anxiety to the already harassed life of the New England farmer.

BLACK-EYED SUSAN
Rudbeckia hirta

BUSH-HONEYSUCKLE.

Diervilla lonicera. Honeysuckle Family.

An upright shrub from one to four feet high. *Leaves.* — Opposite; oblong; taper-pointed. *Flowers.* — Yellow, sometimes much tinged with red; clustered usually in threes in the axils of the upper leaves and at the summit of the stem.

This pretty little shrub is found along our rocky hills and mountains. The blossoms appear in early summer, and form a good example of nectar-bearing flowers. The lower lobe of the corolla is crested and more deeply colored than the others, thus advising the bee of secreted treasure. The hairy filaments of the stamens are so

BUSH-HONEYSUCKLE *Diervilla lonicera*

placed as to protect the nectar from injury by rain. When the blossom has been despoiled and at the same time fertilized, for the nectar-seeking bee has probably deposited some pollen upon its pistil, the color of the corolla changes from a pale to a deep yellow, thus giving warning to the insect-world that further attentions would be useless to both parties.

TOUCH-ME-NOT. JEWELWEED.
Touch-me-not Family.

Impatiens pallida. Pale Jewelweed.

Flowers. — Pale yellow, somewhat spotted with reddish brown; common northward.

Impatiens capensis. Spotted Jewelweed.

Flowers. — Orange-yellow, spotted with reddish brown; common southward.

These beautiful plants are found along shaded streams and marshes, and are profusely hung with brilliant jewel-like flowers during the summer months. In the later year they bear those closed inconspicuous blossoms which fertilize in the bud and are called cleistogamous flowers. The jewelweed has begun to appear along the English rivers, and it is said that the ordinary showy blossoms are comparatively rare, while the cleistogamous ones abound. Does not this look almost like a determination on the part of the plant to secure a firm foothold in its new environment before expending its energy on flowers which, though radiant and attractive, are quite dependent on insect-visitors for fertilization and perpetuation?

The name touch-me-not refers to the seed-pods, which burst open with such violence when touched, as to project their seeds to a comparatively great distance. This ingenious mechanism secures the dispersion of the seeds without the aid of the wind or animals. In parts of New York the plant is called "silver-leaf," from its silvery appearance when touched with rain or dew, or when held beneath the water.

YELLOW FRINGED ORCHIS. ORANGE ORCHIS.

Habenaria ciliaris. Orchid Family.

Stem. — Leafy; one to two feet high. *Leaves.* — The lower oblong to lance-shaped; the upper passing into pointed bracts. *Flowers.* — Deep orange color, with a slender spur and deeply fringed lip; growing in an oblong spike.

Years may pass without our meeting this the most brilliant of our orchids. Suddenly one August day we chance upon just such a boggy meadow as we have searched in vain a hundred times, and behold myriads of its deep orange, dome-like spires erecting themselves in radiant beauty over whole acres of land. The separate flowers, with their long spurs and deeply fringed lips, will repay a close examination. They are well calculated, massed in such brilliant clusters, to arrest the attention of whatever insects may specially affect them. Although I have watched many of these plants I have never seen an insect visit one, and am inclined to think that they are fertilized by night moths.

Mr. Baldwin declares: "If I ever write a romance of Indian life, my dusky heroine, Birch Tree or Trembling Fawn, shall meet her lover with a wreath of this orchis on her head."

ELECAMPANE.

Inula helenium. Composite Family.

Stem. — Stout; three to five feet high. *Leaves.* — Alternate; large; woolly beneath; the upper partly clasping. *Flower-heads.* — Yellow; large; composed of both ray and disk-flowers.

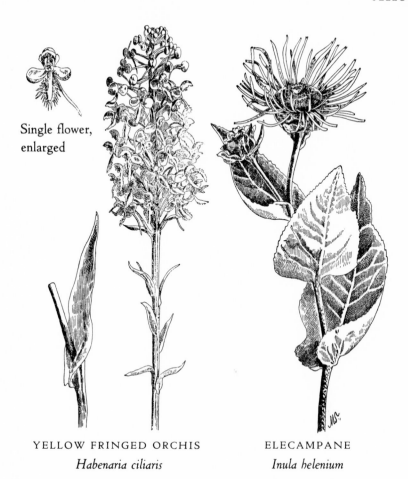

Single flower,
enlarged

YELLOW FRINGED ORCHIS
Habenaria ciliaris

ELECAMPANE
Inula helenium

When we see these great yellow disks peeping over the pasture walls or flanking the country lanes, we feel that midsummer is at its height. Flowers are often subservient courtiers, and make acknowledgment of whatever debt they owe by that subtlest of flatteries — imitation. Did not the blossoms of the dawning year frequently wear the livery of the snow which had thrown its protecting mantle over their first efforts? And these new-comers — whose gross, rotund countenances so clearly betray the results of high living — do not they pay their respects to their great benefactor after the same fashion? — with the result that a myriad miniature suns shine upward from meadow and roadside.

The stout, mucilaginous root of this plant is valued by farmers as a horse-medicine, especially in epidemics of epizootic, one of its common names in England being horse-heal.

In ancient times the elecampane was considered an important stimulant to the human brain and stomach, and it was mentioned as such over two thousand years ago in the writings of Hippocrates, the "Father of Medicine."

The common name is supposed to be a corruption of *ala Campania,* and refers to the frequent occurrence of the plant in that ancient province of Southern Italy.

YELLOW SWEET CLOVER. YELLOW MELILOT.

Melilotus officinalis. Pea Family.

Two to four feet high. *Stem.* – Upright. *Leaves.* — Divided into three toothed leaflets. *Flowers.* — Yellow; growing in spike-like racemes.

This plant is found blossoming along the roadsides in summer. It was formerly called in England "king's-clover," because as Parkinson writes, "the yellowe flowers doe crown the top of the stalks." The leaves become fragrant in drying.

Fireweed
Epilobium angustifolium
(page 194)

Wood Lily
Lilium philadelphicum
(page 217)

Black Cohosh
Cimicifuga racemosa
(page 46)

Wild Geranium
Geranium maculatum
(page 233)

White Sweet Clover
Melilotus alba
(page 59)

Evening-Primrose
Oenothera biennis
(page 133)

ROADSIDE FLOWERS

EVENING-PRIMROSE.

Oenothera biennis. Evening-primrose Family.

Stout; erect; one to five feet high. *Leaves.* — Alternate; lance-shaped to oblong. *Flowers.* — Pale yellow; in a leafy spike; opening at night.

Along the roadsides in midsummer we notice a tall, rank-growing plant, which seems chiefly to bear buds and faded blossoms. And unless we are already familiar with the owl-like tendencies of the evening-primrose, we are surprised, some dim twilight, to find this same plant resplendent with a mass of fragile yellow flowers, which are exhaling their faint delicious fragrance on the evening air.

EVENING-PRIMROSE
Oenothera biennis

One brief summer night exhausts the vitality of these delicate blossoms. The faded petals of the following day might serve as a text for a homily against all-night dissipation, did we not know that by its strange habit the evening-primrose guards against the depredations of those myriad insects abroad during the day, which are unfitted to transmit its pollen to the pistil of another flower.

We are impressed by the utilitarianism in vogue in this floral world, as we note that the pale yellow of these blossoms gleams so vividly through the darkness as to advertise effectively their whereabouts, while their fragrance serves as a mute invitation to the pink night-moth, which is their visitor and benefactor. That they change their habits in the late year and remain open during the day is due perhaps to the diminished power of the sun.

STICKTIGHT. BUR-MARIGOLD. BEGGAR-TICKS.

Bidens frondosa. Composite Family.

Two to six feet high. *Stem.* — Branching. *Leaves.* — Opposite; three to five-divided. *Flower-heads.* — Consisting of brownish-yellow tubular flowers; with a leaf-like involucre beneath.

If one were only describing the attractive wild flowers, the sticktight would certainly be omitted, as its appearance is not prepossessing, and the small barbed seed-vessels so cleverly fulfil their destiny in making one's clothes a means of conveyance to "fresh woods and pastures new" as to cause all wayfarers heartily to detest them. "How surely the desmodium growing on some cliff-side, or the bidens on the edge of a pool, prophesy the coming of the traveller, brute or human, that will transport their seeds on his coat," writes Thoreau. But the plant is so constantly encountered in late summer, and yet so generally unknown, that it can hardly be overlooked.

The larger bur-marigold, *B. laevis,* does its best to retrieve the family reputation for ugliness, and surrounds its dingy disk-flowers with a circle of showy golden rays which are strictly decorative,

LARGER BUR-MARIGOLD
Bidens laevis

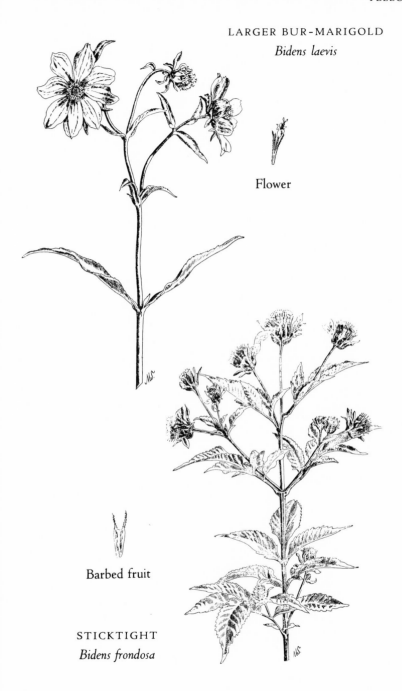

Flower

Barbed fruit

STICKTIGHT
Bidens frondosa

having neither pistils nor stamens, and leaving all the work of the household to the less attractive but more useful disk-flowers. Their effect is pleasing, and late into the autumn the moist ditches look as if sown with gold through their agency. The plant varies in height from six inches to two feet. Its leaves are opposite, lance-shaped, and regularly toothed.

B. cernua, the small bur-marigold, is found often without ray-flowers; when these are present they are shorter than the leaflike involucre which surrounds the flower-head. Its leaves are *irregularly toothed*, and lance-shaped. Its height varies, being anywhere from five inches to three feet.

COMMON MULLEIN.

Verbascum thapsus. Snapdragon Family.

Stems. — Tall and stout; from three to five feet high. *Leaves.* — Oblong; woolly. *Flowers.* — In a long dense spike.

The common mullein is a native of the island of Thapsos, from which it takes its specific name. It was probably brought to this country from Europe by the early colonists, notwithstanding the title of "American velvet plant," which it is rumored to bear in England. The Romans called it "candelaria," from their custom of dipping the long, dried stalk in suet and using it as a funeral torch, and the Greeks utilized the leaves for lamp-wicks. In more modern times they have served as a remedy for the pulmonary complaints of men and beasts alike, "mullein tea" being greatly esteemed by country people. Its especial efficacy with cattle has earned the plant its name of "bullocks' lungwort."

A low rosette of woolly leaves is all that can be seen of the mullein during its first year, the yellow blossoms on their long spikes opening sluggishly about the middle of the second summer. It abounds throughout our dry, rolling meadows, and its tall spires are a familiar feature in the summer landscape.

COMMON MULLEIN
Verbascum thapsus

MOTH MULLEIN
Verbascum blattaria

MOTH MULLEIN.

Verbascum blattaria. Snapdragon Family.

Stem. — Tall and slender. *Leaves.* — Oblong; toothed; the lower sometimes lyre-shaped, the upper partly clasping. *Flowers.* — Yellow or white; tinged with red or purple; in a terminal raceme.

Along the highway from July till October one encounters a slender weed on whose erect stem it would seem as though a number of canary-yellow or purplish-white moths had alighted for a moment's rest. These are the fragile, pretty flowers of the moth mullein, and they are worthy of a closer examination. The reddened or purplish centre of the corolla suggests the probability of hidden nectar, while the pretty tufts of violet wool borne by the stamens are well fitted to protect it from the rain. A little experience of the canny ways of these innocent-looking flowers leads one to ask the wherefore of every new feature.

TALL SUNFLOWER.

Helianthus giganteus. Composite Family.

Stem. — Rough or hairy; from three to ten feet high; branched above. *Leaves.* — Lance-shaped; pointed; rough to the touch, set close to the stem. *Flower-heads.* — Yellow; composed of both ray and disk-flowers.

In late summer many of our lanes are hedged by this beautiful plant, which, like other members of its family, lifts its yellow flowers sunward in pale imitation of the great lifegiver itself.

We have over twenty different species of sunflower.

H. divaricatus is of a lower growth, with opposite, widely spreading leaves and larger flower-heads.

H. annuus is the garden species familiar to all; this is said to be a native of Peru. Mr. Ellwanger* writes regarding it: "In the mythology of the ancient Peruvians it occupied an important place, and was employed as a mystic decoration in ancient Mexican sculpture. Like the lotus of the East, it is equally a sacred and an artistic emblem, figuring in the symbolism of Mexico and Peru, where the Spaniards found it rearing its aspiring stalk in the fields, and serving in the temple as a sign and a decoration, the sun-god's officiating handmaidens wearing upon their breasts representations of the sacred flower in beaten gold."

---

*George Ellwanger, a nineteenth-century American horticulturist.

Gerard describes it as follows: "The Indian Sun, or the golden floure of Peru, is a plant of such stature and talnesse that in one Sommer, being sowne of a seede in April, it hath risen up to the height of fourteen foot in my garden, where one floure was in weight three pound and two ounces, and crosse over-thwart the floure by measure sixteen inches broad."

The generic name is from *helios* — the sun, and *anthos* — a flower.

TALL SUNFLOWER *Helianthus giganteus*

GOLDENROD.

Solidago. Composite Family.

Flower-heads. — Golden-yellow; composed of both ray and disk-flowers.

About eighty species of goldenrod are native to the United States; of these over forty species can be found in our Northeastern States. Many of them are difficult of identification, and it would be useless to describe any but a few of the more conspicuous forms.

A common and noticeable species which flowers early in August is *S. canadensis,* with a tall, stout, rough stem from three to six feet high, lance-shaped leaves, which are usually sharply toothed and pointed, and small flower-heads clustered along the branches which spread from the upper part of the stem.

Another early flowering species is *S. rugosa.* This is a lower plant than *S. canadensis,* with broader leaves.

Still another is the gray goldenrod, *S. nemoralis,* which has a hoary aspect and very bright yellow flowers which are common in dry fields.

S. juncea is also an early bloomer. Its lower leaves are lanceolate or oval, with sharp, spreading teeth and long, winged leaf-stems. The upper ones are narrow and set close to the stem. Its flower-heads grow on the upper side of recurved branches, forming usually a full, spreading cluster.

S. graminifolia has lance-shaped or linear leaves, and flowers which grow in flat-topped clusters, unlike other members of the family; the information that this is a goldenrod often creates surprise, as for some strange reason it seems to be confused with the tansy.

The sweet goldenrod, *S. odora,* is recognized by its narrow, shining, dotted leaves, which when crushed yield a pleasant, permeating fragrance.

The seaside goldenrod, *S. sempervirens,* is a showy, beautiful plant of vigorous habit. Its large, orange-yellow flower-heads, and thick, bright green leaves make brilliant the salt-marshes, sand-hills, and rocky shores of the Atlantic coast every August.

Disk and ray-flowers

LANCE-LEAVED GOLDENROD
Solidago graminifolia

Disk and ray-flowers

SILVERROD *Solidago bicolor*

S. caesia, or blue-stem goldenrod, is a wood-species and among the latest of the year, putting forth its bright clusters for nearly the whole length of its stem long after many of its brethren look like brown wraiths of their former selves.

S. flexicaulis usually has a simple, zigzag stem from one to three feet high, close to which, in the axils of the leaves, the flower-heads are bunched in short clusters. Toward the top of the stem these clusters may be prolonged into a narrow wand. Its leaves are thin, broadly ovate, sharply toothed and pointed at both ends. This plant loves somewhat moist, shaded localities.

The slender, wand-like silverrod, *S. bicolor,* whose partly whitish flower-heads are a departure from the family habit, also survives the early cold and holds its own in the dry woods.

The only species native to Great Britain is *S. virgaurea.*

The generic name, from the Latin, signifies *to make whole,* and refers to the healing properties which have been attributed to the genus.

Seaside Goldenrod
S. sempervirens
(page 140)

Canada Goldenrod
S. canadensis
(page 140)

Rough-stemmed Goldenrod
S. rugosa
(page 140)

Blue-stem Goldenrod
S. caesia
(page 142)

Lance-leaved Goldenrod
S. graminifolia
(page 140)

Early Goldenrod
S. juncea
(page 140)

Zigzag Goldenrod
S. flexicaulis
(page 142)

Silverrod
S. bicolor
(page 142)

Gray Goldenrod
S. nemoralis
(page 140)

GOLDENRODS
Solidago

WITCH HAZEL.

Hamamelis virginiana. Witch Hazel Family.

A tall shrub. *Leaves.* — Oval; wavy-toothed; mostly falling before the flowers appear. *Flowers.* — Honey-yellow; clustered; autumnal. *Fruit.* — A capsule which bursts elastically, discharging its large seeds with vigor.

It seems as though the flowers of the witch hazel were fairly entitled to the "booby-prize" of the vegetable world. Surely no other blossoms make their first appearance so invariably late upon the scene of action. The fringed gentian often begins to open its

WITCH HAZEL
Hamamelis virginiana

"meek and quiet eye" quite early in September. Certain species of goldenrod and aster continue to flower till late in the year, but they began putting forth their bright clusters before the summer was fairly over; while the elusively fragrant, pale yellow blossoms of the witch hazel need hardly be expected till well on in September, when its leaves have fluttered earthward and its fruit has ripened. Does the pleasure which we experience at the spring-like apparition of this leafless yellow-flowered shrub in the autumn woods arise from the same depraved taste which is gratified by strawberries at Christmas, I wonder? Or is it that in the midst of death we have a foretaste of life; a prophecy of the great yearly resurrection which even now we may anticipate?

Thoreau's tastes in such directions were certainly not depraved, and he writes: "The witch hazel loves a hill-side with or without woods or shrubs. It is always pleasant to come upon it unexpectedly as you are threading the woods in such places. Methinks I attribute to it some elfish quality apart from its fame. I love to behold its gray speckled stems." Under another date he writes: "Heard in the night a snapping sound, and the fall of some small body on the floor from time to time. In the morning I found it was produced by the witch-hazel nuts on my desk springing open and casting their seeds quite across my chamber, hard and stony as these nuts were."

The Indians long ago discovered the value of the bark of the witch hazel for medicinal purposes, and it is now utilized in many well-known extracts. The forked branches formerly served as divining rods in the search for water and precious ores. This belief in its mysterious power very possibly arose from its suggestive title, which Dr. Prior says should be spelled *wych* hazel, as it was called after the wych-elm, whose leaves it resembles, and which was so named because the chests termed in old times "wyches" were made of its wood —

> "His hall rofe was full of bacon flytches,
> The chambre charged was with wyches
> Full of egges, butter, and chese."*

---

*Hazlitt's *Early Popular Poetry.*

TANSY.

Tanacetum vulgare. Composite Family.

Stem. — Two to four feet high. *Leaves.* — Divided into toothed leaf-lets. *Flower-heads.* — Yellow; composed of tiny flowers which are nearly, if not all, tubular in shape; borne in flat-topped clusters.

With the name of tansy we seem to catch a whiff of its strong-scented breath and a glimpse of some New England homestead beyond whose borders it has strayed to deck the roadside with its deep yellow, flat topped flower-clusters. The plant has been used in medicine since the Middle Ages, and in more recent times it has been gathered by the country people for "tansy wine" and "tansy

TANSY *Tanacetum vulgare*

tea." In the Roman Church it typifies the bitter herbs which were to be eaten at the Paschal season; and cakes made of eggs and its leaves are called "tansies," and eaten during Lent. It is also frequently utilized in more secular concoctions.

The common name is supposed to be a corruption of the Greek word for *immortality*.

RAGGED FRINGED ORCHIS.

Habenaria lacera. Orchid Family.

Leaves. — Oblong or lance-shaped. *Flowers.* — Greenish or yellowish-white; growing in a spike.

This orchid is found in wet, boggy places during the earlier summer. The lip of the ragged is three-parted, the divisions being deeply fringed, giving what is called in Sweet's "British Flower-Garden"* an "elegantly jagged appearance." So far as superficial beauty and conspicuousness are concerned these flowers do scant justice to the brilliant family to which they belong, and equally excite the scornful exclamation, "You call *that* an orchid!" when brought home for analysis or preservation.

---

*Robert Sweet (1783–1835) was an English naturalist.

SMOOTH FALSE FOXGLOVE.

Gerardia laevigata. Snapdragon Family.

Stem. — Smooth; three to six feet high; usually branching. *Leaves.* — The lower usually deeply incised; the upper narrowly oblong, incised, or entire. *Flowers.* — Yellow; large; in a raceme or spike.

These large, pale yellow flowers are very beautiful and striking when seen in the dry woods of late summer. They are all the more appreciated because there are few flowers abroad at this season

Flower, front view   Flower, side view

RAGGED FRINGED ORCHIS
Habenaria lacera

SMOOTH FALSE FOXGLOVE
Gerardia laevigata

save the Composites, which are decorative and radiant enough, but usually somewhat lacking in the delicate charm we look for in a flower.

For me the plant is associated especially with two localities. One is a mountain-road whose borders, from early June, are brilliant with a show of lovely blossoms, but which, just before the appearance of the false foxglove, is threatened with a dismal break in the floral procession. Only the sharpest eyes are solaced by multitudes of round yellow buds, that burst suddenly into peculiarly fresh and pleasing flowers.

The other favored spot is a wooded island on the coast, surrounded by a salt marsh. In August, when the marsh itself is still brilliant with sea-pinks and milkwort, and beginning to wear its glowing mantle of asters and goldenrods, this island can scarcely boast a blossom save that of the false foxglove. But the plant succeeds in redeeming the lonely spot from any suspicion of dreariness by its lavish display of cheery flowers.

The members of this genus, which is named after Gerard, the author of the famous "Herball," are supposed to be more or less parasitic in their habits, drawing their nourishment from the roots of other plants.

Purple Fringed Orchis
Habenaria fimbriata
(page 241)

Showy Lady's-Slipper
Cypripedium reginae
(page 178)

Yellow Lady's-Slipper
Cypripedium calceolus
(page 108)

Yellow Fringed Orchis
Habenaria ciliaris
(page 128)

White Fringed Orchis
Habenaria blephariglottis
(page 66)

Grass-Pink
Calopogon pulchellus
(page 174)

Arethusa
Arethusa bulbosa
(page 162)

Rose Pogonia
Pogonia ophioglossoides
(page 173)

Pink Lady's-Slipper
Cypripedium acaule
(page 166)

ORCHIDS

Showy Orchis
Orchis spectabilis
(page 165)

III

PINK

TWINFLOWER *Linnaea borealis*

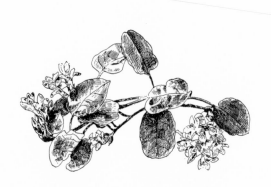

TRAILING ARBUTUS *Epigaea repens*

TWINFLOWER.

Linnaea borealis. Honeysuckle Family.

Stem. — Slender; creeping and trailing. *Leaves.* — Rounded; evergreen. *Flowers.* — Growing in pairs; delicate pink; fragrant; nodding on thread-like, upright flower-stalks.

Whoever has seen

"—beneath dim aisles, in odorous beds,
The slight Linnaea hang its twin-born heads,"

will not soon forget the exquisite carpeting made by its nodding pink flowers, or the delicious perfume which actually filled the air and drew one's attention to the spot from which it was exhaled, tempting one to exclaim, with Richard Jeffries,* "Sweetest of all things is wild-flower air!" That this little plant should have been selected as "the monument of the man of flowers" by the great Linnaeus himself bears testimony to his possession of that appreciation of the beautiful which is supposed to be lacking in men of long scientific training. I believe that there is extant at least one contemporary portrait of Linnaeus in which he wears the tiny flowers in his buttonhole. The rosy twin-blossoms are borne on thread-like, forking flower-stalks, and appear in June in the deep, cool, mossy woods of the North.

TRAILING ARBUTUS. MAYFLOWER. GROUND LAUREL.

Epigaea repens. Heath Family.

Stem. — With rusty hairs; prostrate or trailing. *Leaves.* — Rounded; heart-shaped at base; evergreen. *Flowers.* — Pink; clustered; fragrant.

"Pink, small and punctual,
Aromatic, low,"

describes, but does scant justice to the trailing arbutus, whose waxy

---

*An English author and naturalist (1848–1887).

blossoms and delicious breath are among the earliest prophecies of perfume-laden summer. We look for these flowers in April — not beneath the snow, where tradition rashly locates them, but under the dead brown leaves of last year; and especially among the pines and in light sandy soil. Appearing as they do when we are eager for some tangible assurance that

> "— the Spring comes slowly up this way,"

they win from many of us the gladdest recognition of the year.

In New England they are called Mayflowers, being peddled about the streets of Boston every spring, under the suggestive and loudly emphasized title of "Ply-y-mouth Ma-ayflowers!" Whether they owe this name to the ship which is responsible for so much, or to their season of blooming, in certain localities, might remain an open question had we not the authority of Whittier for attributing it to both causes. In a note prefacing "The Mayflowers," the poet says: "The trailing arbutus or Mayflower grows abundantly in the vicinity of Plymouth, and was the first flower to greet the Pilgrims after their fearful winter." In the poem itself he wonders what the old ship had

> "Within her ice-rimmed bay
> In common with the wild-wood flowers,
> The first sweet smiles of May?"

and continues —

> "Yet 'God be praised!' the Pilgrim said,
> Who saw the blossoms peer
> Above the brown leaves, dry and dead,
> 'Behold our Mayflower here!'

> "God wills it, here our rest shall be,
> Our years of wandering o'er,
> For us the Mayflower of the sea
> Shall spread her sails no more.

> "O sacred flowers of faith and hope,
> As sweetly now as then,
> Ye bloom on many a birchen slope,
> In many a pine-dark glen.

. . .

"So live the fathers in their sons,
　　Their sturdy faith be ours,
And ours the love that overruns
　　Its rocky strength with flowers."

If the poet's fancy was founded on fact, and if our lovely and
widespread Mayflower was indeed the first blossom noted and
christened by our forefathers, it seems as though the problem of a
national flower must be solved by one so lovely and historic as to
silence all dispute. And when we read the following prophetic stan-
zas which close the poem, showing that during another dark period
in our nation's history these brave little blossoms, struggling
through the withered leaves, brought a message of hope and cour-
age to the heroic heart of the Quaker poet, our feeling that they
are peculiarly identified with our country's perilous moments is
intensified.

"The Pilgrims wild and wintry day
　　Its shadow round us draws;
The Mayflower of his stormy bay
　　Our Freedom's struggling cause.

"But warmer suns erelong shall bring
　　To life the frozen sod;
And, through dead leaves of hope, shall spring
　　Afresh the flowers of God!"

SPRING-BEAUTY.

Claytonia virginica. Purslane Family.

Stem. — From a small tuber; often somewhat reclining. *Leaves.* —
Two; opposite; long and narrow. *Flowers.* — White, with pink veins, or
pink with deeper-colored veins; growing in a loose cluster.

"So bashful when I spied her
So pretty, so ashamed!
So hidden in her leaflets

Lest anybody find:
So breathless till I passed her,
So helpless when I turned
And bore her struggling, blushing,
Her simple haunts beyond!
For whom I robbed the dingle,
For whom betrayed the dell,
Many will doubtless ask me,
But I shall never tell!"

Yet we are all free to guess — and what flower — at least in the early year, before it has gained that touch of confidence which it acquires later — is so bashful, so pretty, so flushed with rosy shame, so eager to defend its modesty by closing its blushing petals when carried off by the despoiler — as the spring-beauty? To be sure, she is not "hidden in her leaflets," although often seeking concealment beneath the leaves of other plants — but why not assume that Miss Dickinson has availed herself of something of the license so freely granted to poets — especially, it seems to me, to poets of nature? Perhaps of this class few are more accurate than she, and although we wonder at the sudden blindness which leads her to claim that

"Nature rarer uses yellow
Than another hue —"

when it seems as though it needed but little knowledge of flowers to recognize that yellow, probably, occurs more frequently among them than any other color, and also at the representation of this same nature as

"Spending scarlet like a woman —"

when in reality she is so chary of this splendid hue, still we cannot but appreciate that this poet was in close and peculiar sympathy with flowers, and was wont to paint them with more than customary fidelity.

We look for the spring-beauty in April and May, and often find it in the same moist places — on a brook's edge or skirting the wet woods — as the yellow adder's-tongue. It is sometimes mistaken for an anemone, but its rose-veined corolla and linear leaves easily identify it. One is always glad to discover these children of the country within our city limits, where they can be known and loved by those other children who are so unfortunate as to be denied the knowledge of them in their usual haunts. If the day chances to be cloudy these flowers close and are only induced to open again by an abundance of sunlight. This habit of closing in the shade is common to many flowers, and should be remembered by those who bring home their treasures from the woods and fields, only to discard the majority as hopelessly wilted. If any such exhausted blossoms are placed in the sunlight, with their stems in fresh water, they will probably regain their vigor. Should this treatment fail, an application of very hot — almost boiling — water should be tried. This heroic measure often meets with success.

SPRING-BEAUTY *Claytonia virginica*

ROSE TWISTED-STALK.

Streptopus roseus. Lily Family.

Stems. — Rather stout and zigzag; forking and diverging. *Leaves.* — Taper-pointed; slightly clasping. *Flowers.* — Dull purplish-pink; hanging on thread-like flower stalks from the axils of the leaves. *Fruit.* — Red; roundish; late summer.

This plant presents a graceful group of forking branches and pointed leaves. No blossom is seen from above, but on picking a branch one finds beneath each of its outspread leaves one or two slender, bent stalks from which hang the pink, bell-like flowers. In general aspect the plant somewhat resembles its relation, the Solomon's-seal, with which it is found blossoming in the woods of May or June. The English title is a translation of the generic name, *Streptopus.*

In August one finds the curved leafy stems hung with bright red berries.

WILD PINK.

Silene caroliniana var. *pensylvanica.* Pink Family.

Stems. — Four to eight inches high. *Leaves.* — Those from the root narrowly wedge-shaped; those on the stem lance-shaped, opposite. *Flowers.* — Bright pink; clustered.

When a vivid cluster of wild pinks gleams from some rocky opening in the May woods, it is difficult to restrain one's eagerness, for there is something peculiarly enticing in these fresh, vigorous-looking flowers. They are quite unlike most of their fragile contemporaries, for already they seem imbued with the glowing warmth of summer, and to have no memory of that snowy past which appears to leave its imprint on so many blossoms of the early year.

In waste places, from June until September or later, we find the small clustered pink flowers, which open transiently in the sunshine, of the sleepy catchfly, *S. antirrhina.*

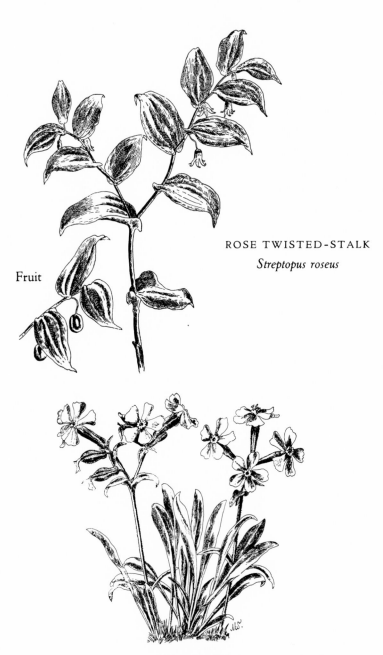

Fruit

ROSE TWISTED-STALK
Streptopus roseus

WILD PINK *Silene caroliniana* var. *pensylvanica*

ARETHUSA.

Arethusa bulbosa. Orchid Family.

Scape. — Sheathed; from a globular bulb; usually one-flowered. *Leaf.* — "Solitary; linear; nerved; hidden in the sheaths of the scape; protruding after flowering." (Gray.) *Flower.* — Rose-purple; large; with a bearded lip.

In some localities this beautiful flower is very plentiful. Every June will find certain New England marshes tinged with its rose-purple blossoms, while in other near and promising bogs it may be sought vainly for years. At least it may be hoped for in wet places as far south as North Carolina, its most favorite haunt being perhaps a cranberry-swamp. Concerning it, Mr. Burroughs writes: "Arethusa was one of the nymphs who attended Diana, and was by that goddess turned into a fountain, that she might escape the god of the river Alpheus, who became desperately in love with her on seeing her at her bath. Our Arethusa is one of the prettiest of the orchids, and has been pursued through many a marsh and quaking-bog by her lovers. She is a bright pink-purple flower, an inch or more long, with the odor of sweet violets. The sepals and petals rise up and arch over the column, which we may call the heart of the flower, as if shielding it. In Plymouth County, Mass., where the Arethusa seems common, I have heard it called Indian pink."

Common Mullein
Verbascum thapsus
(page 136)

Tall Sunflower
Helianthus giganteus
(page 138)

Moth Mullein
Verbascum blattaria
(page 137)

Butterfly-Weed
Asclepias tuberosa
(page 218)

Bouncing Bet
Saponaria officinalis
(page 206)

Ground-Cherry
Physalis virginiana
(page 77)

Scarlet Pimpernel
Anagallis arvensis
(page 224)

FIELDS

SHOWY ORCHIS.

Orchis spectabilis. Orchid Family.

Stem. — Four-angled; with leaf-life bracts; rising from fleshy, fibrous roots. *Leaves.* — Two; oblong; shining; three to six inches long. *Flowers.* — In a loose spike; purple-pink, the lower lip white.

This flower not only charms us with its beauty when its clusters begin to dot the rich May woods, but interests us as being usually the first member of the Orchid family to appear upon the scene; although it is claimed in certain localities that the beautiful Calypso always, and the Indian moccasin occasionally, precedes it.

A certain fascination attends the very name of orchid. Botanist and unscientific flower-lover alike pause with unwonted interest when the discovery of one is announced. With the former there is always the possibility of finding some rare species, while the ex-

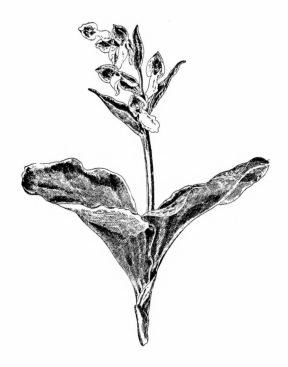

SHOWY ORCHIS *Orchis spectabilis*

citement of the latter is apt to be whetted with the hope of behold-
ing a marvellous imitation of bee or butterfly fluttering from a
mossy branch with roots that draw their nourishment from the air!
While this little plant is sure to fail of satisfying the hopes of either,
it is far prettier if less rare than many of its brethren, and its
interesting mechanism will repay our patient study. It is said closely
to resemble the "long purples," *O. mascula,* which grew near the
scene of Ophelia's tragic death.

PALE CORYDALIS.

Corydalis sempervirens. Poppy Family.

Stem. — Six inches to two feet high. *Leaves.* — Pale; divided into
delicate leaflets. *Flowers.* — Pink and yellow; in loose clusters.

From rocky clefts in the early summer woods springs the pale
corydalis, its graceful foliage dim with a whitish bloom, and its
delicate, rosy, yellow-tipped flowers betraying, by their odd, flat
corollas, their kinship with the Dutchman's-breeches and squirrel-
corn of the early year, as well as with the bleeding-hearts of the
garden. Thoreau assigns them to the middle of May, and says they
are "rarely met with," which statement does not coincide with the
experience of those who find the rocky woodlands each summer
abundantly decorated with their fragile clusters.

The generic name, *Corydalis,* is the ancient Greek title for the
crested lark, and is said to refer to the crested seeds of this genus.

PINK LADY'S-SLIPPER. MOCCASIN-FLOWER.

Cypripedium acaule. Orchid Family.

Scape. — Eight to twelve inches high; two-leaved at base; downy;
one-flowered. *Leaves.* — Two; large; many-nerved and plaited; sheathing
at the base. *Flowers.* — Solitary; the pink, veiny lip, an inflated pouch;
sepals and petals greenish and spreading.

PALE CORYDALIS
Corydalis sempervirens

PINK LADY'S-SLIPPER
Cypripedium acaule

> "Graceful and tall the slender, drooping stem,
>   With two broad leaves below,
> Shapely the flower so lightly poised between,
>   And warm her rosy glow."

writes Elaine Goodale* of the moccasin-flower. This is a blossom whose charm never wanes. It seems to be touched with the spirit of the deep woods, and there is a certain fitness in its Indian name, for it looks as though it came direct from the home of the red man. All who have found it in its secluded haunts will sympathize with Mr. Higginson's** feeling that each specimen is a rarity, even though he should find a hundred to an acre. Gray assigned it to "dry or moist woods," while Mr. Baldwin writes: "The finest specimens I ever saw sprang out of cushions of crisp reindeer moss high up among the rocks of an exposed hill-side, and again I have found it growing vigorously in almost open swamps, but nearly colorless from excessive moisture." The same writer quotes a lady who is familiar with it in the Adirondacks. She says: "It seems to have a great fondness for decaying wood, and I often see a whole row perched like birds along a crumbling log;" while I recall a mountain lake where the steep cliffs rise from the water's edge; here and there, on a tiny shelf strewn with pine-needles, can be seen a pair of large veiny leaves, above which, in early June, the pink balloon-like blossom floats from its slender scape.

RACEMED MILKWORT.

Polygala polygama. Milkwort Family.

Stems. — Very leafy; six to nine inches high; with cleistogamous flowers on underground runners. *Leaves.* — Lance-shaped or oblong. *Flowers.* — Purple-pink; loosely clustered in a terminal raceme.

Like its more attractive sister, the fringed polygala, this little plant hides its most useful, albeit unattractive, blossoms in the ground, where they can fulfil their destiny of perpetuating the spe-

---

*An American poet (1863–1953).
**Thomas Wentworth Higginson, a Massachusetts author (1823–1911).

cies without danger of molestation by thievish insects or any of the distractions incidental to a more worldly career. Exactly what purpose the little above-ground flowers, which appear so plentifully in sandy soil in July, are intended to serve, it is difficult to understand.

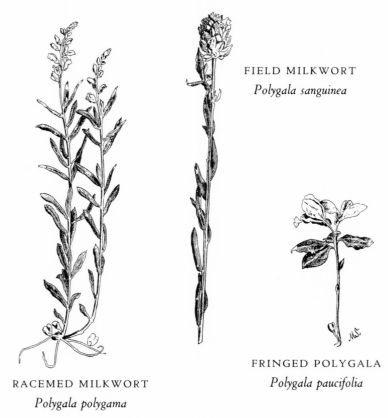

FIELD MILKWORT
Polygala sanguinea

FRINGED POLYGALA
Polygala paucifolia

RACEMED MILKWORT
Polygala polygama

FIELD MILKWORT.

Polygala sanguinea. Milkwort Family.

Stem. — Six inches to a foot high; sparingly branched above; leafy to the top. *Leaves.* — Oblong-linear. *Flowers.* — Growing in round or oblong heads which are somewhat clover-like in appearance; bright pink or almost red, occasionally paler.

This pretty little plant abounds in moist and also sandy places, growing on mountain heights as well as in the salt meadows which skirt the area. In late summer its bright flower-heads gleam vividly through the grasses, and from their form and color might almost be mistaken for pink clover. Occasionally they are comparatively pale and inconspicuous.

FRINGED POLYGALA.

Polygala paucifolia. Milkwort Family.

Flowering-stems. — Three or four inches high, from long, prostrate or underground shoots which also bear cleistogamous flowers. *Leaves.* — The lower, small and scale-like, scattered; the upper, ovate, and crowded at the summit. *Flowers.* — Purple-pink, rarely white; rather large.

"I must not forget to mention that delicate and lovely flower of May, the fringed polygala. You gather it when you go for the fragrant showy orchis — that is, if you are lucky enough to find it. It is rather a shy flower, and is not found in every wood. One day we went up and down through the woods looking for it — woods of mingled oak, chestnut, pine, and hemlock — and were about giving it up when suddenly we came upon a gay company of them beside an old wood-road. It was as if a flock of small rose-purple butterflies had alighted there on the ground before us. The whole plant has a singularly fresh and tender aspect. Its foliage is of a slightly purple tinge and of very delicate texture. Not the least interesting feature about the plant is the concealed fertile flower which it bears on a subterranean stem, keeping, as it were, one flower for beauty and one for use."

It seems unnecessary to tempt "odorous comparisons" by endeavoring to supplement the above description of Mr. Burroughs.

	EARLY FALL	Wild Carrot
Common Milkweed	Purple Gerardia	*Daucus carota*
Asclepias syriaca	*Gerardia purpurea*	(page 73)
(page 181)	(page 200)	
White Snakeroot	Common Cinquefoil	Rattlesnake-Plantain
Eupatorium rugosum	*Potentilla canadensis*	*Goodyera pubescens*
(page 80)	(page 114)	(page 60)

ROSE POGONIA. SNAKE-MOUTH.

Pogonia ophioglossoides. Orchid Family.

Stem. — Six to nine inches high; from a fibrous root. *Leaves.* — An oval or lance-oblong one near the middle of the stem, and a smaller or bract-like one near the terminal flower, occasionally one or two others, with a flower in their axils. *Flower.* — Pale pink, sometimes white; sweet-scented; one inch long; lip bearded and fringed.

Mr. Baldwin maintains that there is no wild flower of as pure a pink as this unless it be the *Sabbatia.* Its color has also been described as a "peach-blossom red." As already mentioned, the plant is found blossoming in bogs during the early summer in company with the *Calopogons* and sundews. Its violet-like fragrance greatly enhances its charm.

The botanists have great difficulty at times in describing the colors of certain flowers, and when the blossoms look to one eye pink, to another purple, they compromise and give the color as "pink-purple." It has been no easy matter to settle satisfactorily the positions in this book of many of the flowers, more especially as the individuals vary constantly in depth of color, and even in actual color.

July 7, 1852, Thoreau devotes a page in his journal to some of these doubtful-colored flowers, whose heathenish titles excite his ire. "Pogonias are still abundant in the meadows, but arethusas I have not lately seen. . . . The very handsome 'pink-purple' flowers of the *Calopogon pulchellus* enrich the grass all around the edge of Hubbard's blueberry swamp, and are now in their prime. The *Arethusa bulbosa,* 'crystalline purple,' *Pogonia ophioglossoides,* snake-mouthed (tongued) arethusa, 'pale purple,' and the *Calopogon pulchellus,* grass pink, 'pink-purple,' make one family in my mind (next to the purple orchis, or with it), being flowers *par excellence,* all flowers, naked flowers, and difficult, at least the calopogon, to preserve. But they are flowers, excepting the first, at least, without a name. Pogonia! Calopogon! They would blush still deeper if they knew the names man has given them. . . . The pogonia has a strong snaky odor. The first may perhaps retain its name, arethusa, from the places in which it grows, and the other two deserve the names of nymphs, perhaps of the class called Naiades. . . . To be sure, in a perfect flower there will be proportion between the flowers and leaves, but these are fair and delicate, nymph-like."

LARGE CRANBERRY.

Vaccinium macrocarpon. Heath Family.

Stems. — Slender; trailing; one to four feet long. *Leaves.* — Oblong; obtuse; whitened beneath. *Flowers.* — Pale pink; nodding. *Fruit.* — A large, acid, red berry.

In the peat-bogs of our Northeastern States we may look in June for the pink nodding flowers, and in late summer for the large red berries of this well-known and useful plant.

The small cranberry, *V. oxycoccus,* bears a much smaller fruit. Its ovate, acute leaves have strongly revolute margins and are whitish beneath. The acid berries are edible when cooked.

The mountain-cranberry, *V. vitis-idaea,* is found along the coast and mountains of New England, inland to Lake Superior and far northward. Its smooth, shining, obovate leaves also have revolute margins. Below they are dotted with black, bristly points. The blossoms grow in short terminal clusters. These berries also are smaller than those of the common cranberry.

GRASS-PINK.

Calopogon pulchellus. Orchid Family.

Scape. — Rising about one foot from a small solid bulb. *Leaf.* — Linear; grass-like. *Flowers.* — Two to six on each scape; purple-pink; about one inch broad; the lip as if hinged at its insertion, bearded toward the summit with white, yellow, and purple hairs. The peculiarity of this orchid is that the ovary is not twisted, and consequently the lip is on the upper instead of the lower side of the flower.

In the bogs of early summer, side by side with the glistening sundew, and the delicate snake-mouth, one finds these lovely flowers.

ROSE POGONIA
Pogonia ophioglossoides

GRASS-PINK
Calopogon pulchellus

LARGE CRANBERRY *Vaccinium macrocarpon*

I remember well the first time I ever saw the *Calopogon* at home (for previously specimens had been sent to me). It was one morning late in June, while taking a walk with a friend and her little girl. We had just crossed a wet meadow, bright with the fronds of the *Osmunda,* the rank foliage of the false hellebore, and the canary-yellow of the day-blooming evening-primrose. As we reached the comparatively firm ground which skirted the woods, our eyes fell upon a patch of feathery grasses and radiant *Calopogons.*

Knowing only too well the childish instinct immediately to rush upon such a mass of floral loveliness, my first thought was to shield with outstretched arms the delicate beauties, hesitating to pick even a single blossom until we had feasted our eyes, for a time at least, upon their unruffled grace.

After all, how much better than to bear away a burden of blossoms, which nearly always seem to leave half their beauty behind them, is it to retain a memory of some enchanted spot unrifled of its charm.

Then, too, the prevalent lack of sense of self-restraint in the picking and uprooting of flowers and ferns is resulting in the extermination of many valuable species. This is especially true in the case of orchids. It is devoutly to be wished that every true lover of our woods and fields would set his face sternly against the ruthless habit, regardless of the pleas that may be offered in excuse.

This picking and uprooting tendency does not begin to threaten as seriously the future of our really common flowers (some of which, by the way, are so unprincipled themselves as almost to deserve extermination) as it does that of our rarer and more beautiful species. Many of these will disappear from the country, it is to be feared, if some counter-influence is not exerted, and if it is not remembered that in the case of annuals and biennials as much injury may be done to a species by the picking of the seed-yielding flower as by the uprooting of the plant itself.

SHEEP LAUREL. LAMBKILL.

Kalmia angustifolia. Heath Family.

A shrub from one to three feet high. *Leaves.* — Narrowly oblong; light green. *Flowers.* — Deep pink; in lateral clusters.

This low shrub grows abundantly with the mountain laurel, bearing smaller deep pink flowers at the same season, and narrower, paler leaves. It is said to be the most poisonous of the genus, and to be especially deadly to sheep, while deer are supposed to feed upon its leaves with impunity.

The flower is one of Thoreau's favorites. In his journal, June

13, 1852, he writes: "Lambkill is out. I remember with what delight I used to discover this flower in dewy mornings. All things in this world must be seen with the morning dew on them, must be seen with youthful, early opened, hopeful eyes."

And two years later, oddly enough on the same day of the month, he finds them equally admirable at the approach of "dewy eve." "How beautiful the solid cylinders of the lambkill now just before sunset; small ten-sided rosy-crimson basins, about two inches above the recurved, drooping, dry capsules of last year, and sometimes those of the year before, two inches lower."

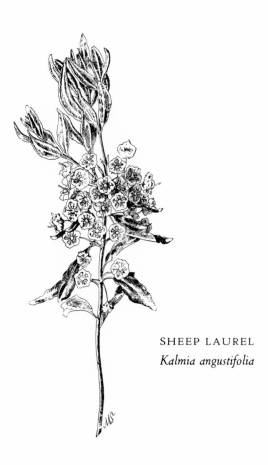

SHEEP LAUREL
Kalmia angustifolia

SHOWY LADY'S-SLIPPER.

Cypripedium reginae. Orchid Family.

Stems. — Downy; two feet high. *Leaves.* — Large; ovate; pointed; plaited. *Flowers.* — Large; the three sepals and two lateral petals, white; the lip white, pink in front, much inflated.

My eager hunts for this, the most beautiful of our orchids, have never been crowned with success.* But once I saw a fresh cluster

*Since writing the above I have tracked it to its home.

SHOWY LADY'S-SLIPPER
Cypripedium reginae

of these lovely flowers in a friend's house, and regaled myself with their rich, stately beauty and delicious fragrance. Strangely enough I find no mention of this latter quality either in Gray or in Mr. Baldwin's work on orchids.

Mr. Baldwin describes the lip of this flower as "crimped, shell-shaped, varying from a rich pink-purple blotched with white to pure white." He says that in southern Connecticut it may be found by the 20th of June, but that the White Mountains rarely afford it before July. It is due in the Berkshires, Mass., late in June.

It grows in peat-bogs, and its height and foliage strongly suggest the false hellebore.

This flower is one of a species whose life is threatened owing to the oft-lamented ruthlessness of the "flower-picker."

Near Lenox, Mass., there is one locality where the showy lady's-slipper can be found. Fortunately, one would suppose, this spot is known only to a few; but as one of the few who possess the secret is a country boy who *uproots these plants and sells them by the dozen* in Lenox and Pittsfield, the time is not distant when the flower will no longer be found in the shadowy silences of her native haunts, but only, robbed of half her charm, languishing in stiff rows along the garden-path.

PINK AZALEA. WILD HONEYSUCKLE.
PINXTER-FLOWER.

Rhododendron nudiflorum. Heath Family.

A shrub from two to six feet high. *Leaves.* — Narrowly oblong; downy underneath; usually appearing somewhat later than the flowers. *Flowers.* — Pink; clustered.

Our May swamps and moist woods are made rosy by masses of the pink azalea, which is often known as the wild honeysuckle, although not even a member of the Honeysuckle family. It is in the height of its beauty before the blooming of the laurel, and heralds the still lovelier pageant which is even then in rapid course of preparation.

PINK AZALEA
Rhododendron nudiflorum

In the last century the name of Mayflower was given to the shrub by the Swedes in the neighborhood of Philadelphia. Peter Kalm, the pupil of Linnaeus, after whom our laurel, *Kalmia,* is named, writes the following description of the shrub in his "Travels," which were published in English in 1771, and which explains the origin of one of its titles: "Some of the Swedes and Dutch call them Pinxter-bloom (Whitsunday-flower), as they really are in bloom about Whitsuntide; and at a distance they have some similarity to the Honeysuckle or 'Lonicera.' ... Its flowers were now open and added a new ornament to the woods.... They sit in a circle round the stem's extremity and have either a dark red or a lively red color; but by standing for some time the sun bleaches them, and at last they get to a whitish hue.... They have some smell, but I cannot say it is very pleasant. However, the beauty of the flowers entitles them to a place in every flower-garden." While our pink azalea could hardly be called "dark red" under any circumstances, it varies greatly in the color of its flowers.

The azalea is the national flower of Flanders.

COMMON MILKWEED.

Asclepias syriaca. Milkweed Family.

Stem. — Tall; stout; downy; with a milky juice. *Leaves.* — Generally opposite or whorled; the upper sometimes scattered; large; oblong; pale; minutely downy underneath. *Flowers.* — Dull purplish-pink; clustered at

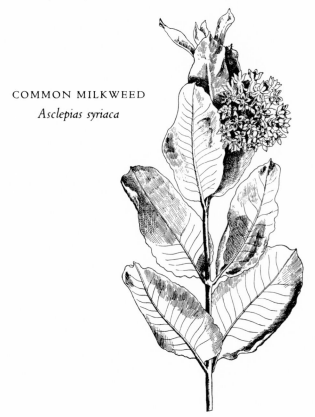

COMMON MILKWEED
Asclepias syriaca

the summit and along the sides of the stem. *Fruit.* — Two pods, one of which is large and full of silky-tufted seeds, the other often stunted.

This is probably the commonest representative of this striking and beautiful native family. The tall, stout stems, large, pale leaves, dull pink clustered flowers which appear in July, and later the puffy pods filled with the silky-tufted seeds beloved of imaginative children, are familiar to nearly everyone who spends a portion of the year in the country. The young sprouts are said to make an excellent pot-herb; the silky hairs of the seed-pods have been used for the stuffing of pillows and mattresses, and can be mixed with flax or wool and woven to advantage; while paper has been manufactured from the stout stalks.

The four-leaved milkweed, *A. quadrifolia,* is the most delicate member of the family, with fragrant rose-tinged flowers which appear on the dry wooded hill-sides quite early in June, and slender stems which are usually leafless below, and with one or two whorls and one or two pairs of oval, taper-pointed leaves above.

The swamp-milkweed, *A. incarnata,* grows commonly in moist places. Its very leafy stems are two or three feet high, with narrowly oblong, pointed leaves. Its intense purple-pink flowers gleam from the wet meadows nearly all summer. They are smaller than those of the purple milkweed, *A. purpurascens,* which abounds in dry ground, and which may be classed among the deep pink or purple flowers according to the eye of the beholder.

Purple Milkweed
Asclepias purpurascens
(page 182)

Tall Meadow-Rue
Thalictrum polygamum
(page 85)

Canada Lily
Lilium canadense
(page 120)

Meadowsweet
Spiraea latifolia
(page 60)

False Dragonhead
Physostegia virginiana
(page 205)

White Daisy
Chrysanthemum leucanthemum
(page 50)

Shrubby Cinquefoil
Potentilla fruticosa
(page 113)

MEADOWS

SPREADING DOGBANE.

Apocynum androsaemifolium. Dogbane Family.

Stems. — Erect; branching; two or three feet high. *Leaves.* — Opposite; oval. *Flowers.* — Rose-color, veined with deep pink; loosely clustered. *Fruit.* — Two long and slender pods.

The flowers of the dogbane, though small and inconspicuous, are very beautiful if closely examined. The deep pink veining of the corolla suggests nectar, and the insect-visitor is not misled, for at its base are five nectar-bearing glands. The two long, slender seed-pods which result from a single blossom seem inappropriately large, often appearing while the plant is still in flower. Rafinesque*

---

*Constantine Samuel Rafinesque, an American naturalist (1783–1840).

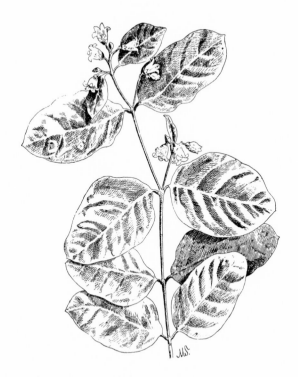

SPREADING DOGBANE *Apocynum androsaemifolium*

states that from the stems may be obtained a thread similar to hemp which can be woven into cloth, from the pods, cotton, and from the blossoms, sugar. Its generic and one of its English titles arose from the belief, which formerly prevailed, that it was poisonous to dogs. The plant is constantly found growing in roadside thickets, with bright, pretty foliage, and blossoms that appear in early summer.

PURPLE-FLOWERING RASPBERRY.

Rubus odoratus. Rose Family.

Stem. — Shrubby, three to five feet high; branching; branches bristly and glandular. *Leaves.* — Three to five-lobed, the middle lobe prolonged. *Flowers.* — Purplish-pink; large and showy; two inches broad. *Fruit.* — Reddish, resembling the garden raspberry.

This flower betrays its relationship to the wild rose, and might easily be mistaken for it, although a glance at the undivided leaves would at once correct such an error. The plant is a decorative one when covered with its showy blossoms, constantly arresting our attention along the wooded roadsides in June and July.

HERB-ROBERT.

Geranium robertianum. Geranium Family.

Stem. — Forking; slightly hairy. *Leaves.* — Three-divided, the divisions again dissected. *Flowers.* — Purple-pink; small.

From June until October many of our shaded woods and glens are abundantly decorated by the bright blossoms of the herb-Robert. The reddish stalks of the plant have won it the name of "redshanks" in the Scotch Highlands. Its strong scent is caused by a resinous secretion which exists in several of the geraniums. In some species this resin is so abundant that the stems will burn like torches, yielding a powerful and pleasant perfume. The common

Fruit

PURPLE-FLOWERING
RASPBERRY
Rubus odoratus

HERB-ROBERT
Geranium robertianum

187

name is said to have been given the plant on account of its supposed virtue in a disease which was known as "Robert's plague," after Robert, Duke of Normandy. In some of the early writers it is alluded to as the "holy herb of Robert."

In fruit the styles of this plant split apart with an elasticity which serves to project the seeds to a distance, it is said, of twenty-five feet.

HEDGE BINDWEED
Convolvulus sepium

HEDGE BINDWEED. WILD MORNING-GLORY.

Convolvulus sepium. Morning-glory Family.

Stem. — Twining or trailing. *Leaves.* — Somewhat arrow-shaped. *Flowers.* — Pink.

Many an unsightly heap of rubbish left by the roadside is hidden by the delicate pink bells of the hedge bindweed, which again will clamber over the thickets that line the streams and about the tumbled stone-wall that marks the limit of the pasture. The pretty flowers at once suggest the morning-glory, to which they are closely allied.

The common European bindweed, *C. arvensis,* has white or pinkish flowers, without bracts beneath the calyx, and a low procumbent or twining stem. It has taken possession of many of our old fields, where it spreads extensively and proves troublesome to farmers.

VIRGINIA MEADOW-BEAUTY. DEERGRASS.

Rhexia virginica. Meadow-beauty Family.

Stem. — Square; with wing-like angles. *Leaves.* — Opposite; narrowly oval. *Flowers.* — Purplish-pink; clustered.

VIRGINIA MEADOW-BEAUTY
Rhexia virginica

It is always a pleasant surprise to happen upon a bright patch of these delicate deep-hued flowers along the marshes or in the sandy fields of midsummer. Their fragile beauty is of that order which causes it to seem natural that they should belong to a genus which is the sole northern representative of a tropical family. In parts of New England they grow in profusion, while in Arkansas the plant is said to be a great favorite with the deer, hence one of its common names. The flower has been likened to a scarlet evening-primrose, and there is certainly a suggestion of the evening-primrose in the four rounded, slightly heart-shaped petals. The protruding stamens, with their long yellow anthers, are conspicuous.

Of the plant in the late year Thoreau writes: "The scarlet leaves and stems of the rhexia, sometime out of flower, make almost as bright a patch in the meadows now as the flowers did. Its seed-vessels are perfect little cream-pitchers of graceful form."

DEPTFORD PINK.

Dianthus armeria. Pink Family.

One to two feet high. *Leaves.* — Opposite; long and narrow; hairy. *Flowers.* — Pink, with white dots; clustered.

In July and August we find these little flowers in our Eastern fields. The generic name, which signifies *Jove's own flower,* hardly applies to these inconspicuous blossoms. Perhaps it was originally bestowed upon *D. caryophyllus,* a large and fragrant English member of the genus, which was the origin of our garden carnation.

Broad-leaved Aster A. macrophyllus (page 252)	Late Purple Aster A. patens (page 252)	Purple-stemmed Aster A. puniceus (page 253)
Heart-leaved Aster A. cordifolius (page 253)	Seaside Purple Aster A. spectabilis (page 254) ASTERS	New England Aster A. novae-angliae (page 252)

SPOTTED JOE-PYE-WEED. TRUMPET-WEED.

Eupatorium maculatum. Composite Family.

Stem. — Stout and tall; two to twelve feet high; often dotted. *Leaves.* — In whorls of three to six; oblong or oval; pointed; rough; veiny; toothed. *Flower-heads.* — Purplish-pink; small; composed entirely of tubular blossoms, with long protruding styles; growing in large clusters at or near the summit of the stem.

The summer is nearly over when the tall, conspicuous Joe-Pye-weeds begin to tinge with "crushed raspberry" the lowlands through which we pass. In parts of the country it is nearly as common as the goldenrods and asters which appear at about the same season. With the deep purple of the ironweed it gives variety to the intense hues which herald the coming of autumn.

"Joe Pye" is said to have been the name of an Indian who cured typhus fever in New England by means of this plant. The tiny trumpet-shaped blossoms which make up the flower-heads may have suggested the other common name.

JOE-PYE-WEED
Eupatorium maculatum

FIREWEED. GREAT WILLOW-HERB.

Epilobium angustifolium. Evening-primrose Family.

Stem. — Four to seven feet high. *Leaves.* — Scattered; lance-shaped; willow-like. *Flowers.* — Purplish-pink; large; in a long raceme the upper part of which is often nodding. *Fruit.* — A pod with silky-tufted seeds.

In midsummer this striking plant begins to mass its deep-hued blossoms along the roadsides and low meadows. It is supposed to flourish with especial abundance in land that has newly been burned over; hence, its common name of fireweed. Its willow-like foliage has given it its other English title. The likeness between the blossoms of this plant and those of the evening-primrose betray their kinship. When the stamens of the fireweed first mature and discharge their pollen the still immature style is curved backward and downward with its stigmas closed. Later it straightens and lengthens to its full dimensions, so spreading its four stigmas as to be in position to receive the pollen of another flower from the visiting bee.

PURPLE LOOSESTRIFE. SPIKED LOOSESTRIFE.

Lythrum salicaria. Loosestrife Family.

Stem. — Tall and slender; four-angled. *Leaves.* — Lance-shaped, with a heart-shaped base; sometimes whorled in threes. *Flowers.* — Deep purple-pink; crowded and whorled in an interrupted spike.

One who has seen an inland marsh in August aglow with this beautiful plant is almost ready to forgive the Old Country some of the many pests she has shipped to our shores in view of this radiant acquisition. The botany locates it anywhere between Nova Scotia and Delaware. It may be seen in the perfection of its beauty along the marshy shores of the Hudson and in the swamps of the Wallkill Valley.

When we learn that these flowers are called "long purples" by the English country people, the scene of Ophelia's tragic death rises before us:

FIREWEED
Epilobium angustifolium

PURPLE LOOSESTRIFE
Lythrum salicaria

"There is a willow grows aslant a brook,
That shows his hoar leaves in the glassy stream,
There with fantastic garlands did she come,
Of crow-flowers, nettles, daisies, and long purples
That liberal shepherds give a grosser name,
But our cold maids do dead men's fingers call them."

Dr. Prior, however, says that it is supposed that Shakespeare intended to designate the purple flowering orchis, *O. mascula,* which is said closely to resemble the showy orchis of our spring woods.

The flowers of the purple loosestrife are especially interesting to botanists on account of their *trimorphism,* which word signifies *occurring in three forms,* and refers to the stamens and pistils, which vary in size in the different blossoms, being of three different lengths, the pollen from any given set of stamens being especially fitted to fertilize a pistil of corresponding length.

SEA-PINK. MARSH-PINK.

Sabatia stellaris. Gentian Family.

Stem. — Slender; loosely branched. *Leaves.* — Opposite; oblong to lance-shaped; the upper narrowly linear. *Flowers.* — Large; deep pure pink to almost white.

The advancing year has few fairer sights to show us than a salt meadow flushed with these radiant blossoms. They are so abundant, so deep-hued, so delicate! One feels tempted to lie down among the pale grasses and rosy stars in the sunshine of the August morning and drink his fill of their beauty. How often nature tries to the utmost our capacity of appreciation and leaves us still insatiate! At such times it is almost a relief to turn from the mere contemplation of beauty to the study of its structure; it rests our overstrained faculties.

The vivid coloring and conspicuous marking of these flowers indicate that they aim to attract certain members of the insect world. As in the fireweed the pistil of the freshly opened blossom

SEA-PINK
Sabatia stellaris

is curved sideways, with its lobes so closed and twisted as to be inaccessible on their stigmatic surfaces to the pollen which the already mature stamens are discharging. When the effete anthers give evidence that they are *hors de combat* by their withered appearance, the style erects itself and spreads its stigmas.

Many of our readers will be interested in the following information, copied from "Garden and Forest," as to the tradition in Plymouth concerning the scientific name of this genus:

"No more beautiful flower grows in New England than the *Sabbatia*, and at Plymouth, where it is especially profuse and luxuriant on the borders of the ponds so characteristic of that part of eastern Massachusetts, it is held in peculiar affection and, one may almost say, reverence. It is locally called 'the rose of Plymouth,' and during its brief season of bloom is sold in quantities in the streets of the town and used in the adornment of houses and churches. Its name comes from that of an early botanist, Liberatus Sabbatia; but this well-established truth is totally disregarded by local tradition. Almost every one in Plymouth firmly believes that the title is due to the fact that the Pilgrims of 1620 first saw the flower on a Sabbath day, and, entranced by its masses of pinkish lilac-color, named it for the holy day. Indeed, this belief is so deeply ingrained in the Plymouth mind that, we are told, strong objections are made if any other flowers are irreverently mingled with it in church decoration. Yet the legend was invented not more than twenty-five years ago by a man whose identity is still well remembered; and thus it is of even more recent origin than the one, still more universally credited, which says that the Pilgrim Fathers landed upon Plymouth Rock."

ROSE-MALLOW. SWAMP ROSE-MALLOW.

Hibiscus palustris. Mallow Family.

Stem. — Stout and tall; four to eight feet high. *Leaves.* — The lower three-lobed; the upper oblong, whitish and downy beneath. *Flowers.* — Large and showy; pink.

When the beautiful rose-mallow slowly unfolds her pink banner-like petals and admits the eager bee to her stores of golden pollen, then we feel that the summer is far advanced. As truly as the wood-anemone and the bloodroot seem filled with the essence of spring and the promise of the opening year, so does this stately flower glow with the maturity and fulfilment of late summer. Here is none of the timorousness of the early blossoms which peep shyly out, as if ready to beat a hasty retreat should a late frost overtake them, but rather a calm assurance that the time is ripe, and that the salt marshes and brackish ponds are only awaiting their rosy lining.

The marsh mallow, whose roots yield the mucilaginous substance utilized in the well-known confection, is *Althaea officinalis*, an emigrant from Europe. It is a much less common plant than the *Hibiscus,* its pale pink flowers being found in some of the salt marshes of New England and New York.

The common mallow, *Malva neglecta,* which overruns the country dooryards and village waysides, is a little plant with rounded, heart-shaped leaves and small purplish flowers. It is used by the country people for various medicinal purposes and is cultivated and commonly boiled with meat in Egypt. Job pictures himself as being despised by those who had been themselves so destitute as to "cut up mallows by the bushes . . . for their meat."*

---

*Job 30: 4.

ROSE-MALLOW
Hibiscus palustris

MARSH ST. JOHNSWORT.

Hypericum virginicum. St. Johnswort Family.

Stem. — One to two feet high; often pinkish; later bright red. *Leaves.* — Opposite; set close to the stem or clasping by a broad base. *Flowers.* — Pinkish or flesh-color; small; closely clustered at the summit of the stem and in the axils of the leaves.

If one has been so unlucky, from the usual point of view, or so fortunate, looking at the matter with the eyes of the flower-lover, as to find himself in a rich marsh early in August, his eye is likely to fall upon the small, pretty pinkish flowers and pale clasping leaves of the marsh St. Johnswort. A closer inspection will discover that the foliage is dotted with the pellucid glands, and that the stamens are clustered in groups after the family fashion. Should the same marsh be visited a few weeks later, dashes of vivid color will guide one to the spot where the little pink flowers were found. In their place glow the conspicuous ovaries and bright leaves which make the plant very noticeable in late August.

PURPLE GERARDIA.

Gerardia purpurea. Snapdragon Family.

Stem. — One to four feet high; widely branching. *Leaves.* — Linear; sharply pointed. *Flowers.* — Bright purplish-pink; rather large.

In late summer and early autumn these pretty, noticeable flowers brighten the low-lying ground along the coast and in the neighborhood of the Great Lakes. The sandy fields of New England and Long Island are oftentimes a vivid mass of color owing to their delicate blossoms. The plant varies somewhat in the size of its flowers and in the manner of its growth.

The little seaside gerardia, *G. maritima,* is from four inches to a foot high. Its smaller blossoms are also found in salt marshes.

MARSH ST. JOHNSWORT
Hypericum virginicum

PURPLE GERARDIA
Gerardia purpurea

The slender gerardia, *G. tenuifolia,* is common in mountainous regions. The leaves of this species are exceedingly narrow. Like the false foxglove (page 148) and other members of this genus, these plants are supposed to be parasitic in their habits.

SALT-MARSH FLEABANE.

Pluchea purpurascens. Composite Family.

Stem. — Two to five feet high. *Leaves.* — Pale; thickish; oblong or lance-shaped; toothed. *Flower-heads.* — Pink; small; in flat-topped clusters; composed entirely of tubular flowers.

In the salt marshes where we find the starry sea-pinks and the feathery sea-lavender, we notice a pallid-looking plant whose pinkish purple flower-buds are long in opening. It is late summer or autumn before the salt-marsh fleabane is fairly in blossom. There is a strong fragrance to the plant which suggests camphor to some people.

Rose-Mallow
Hibiscus palustris
(page 198)

Smooth False Foxglove
Gerardia laevigata
(page 148)

Marsh Mallow
Althaea officinalis
(page 198)

Salt-Marsh Fleabane
Pluchea purpurascens
(page 202)

Sea-Lavender
Limonium nashii
(page 247)

Marsh St. Johnswort
Hypericum virginicum
(page 200)

Sea-Pink
Sebatia stellaris
(page 196)

Field Milkwort
Polygala sanguinea
(page 169)

Beach Pea
Lathyrus japonicus
(page 249)

SALT MARSH

FALSE DRAGONHEAD.

Physostegia virginiana. Mint Family.

Stems. — Square; upright; wand-like. *Leaves.* — Opposite; sessile; narrow; usually toothed. *Flowers.* — Showy; rose-pink; purple-veined; crowded in terminal leafless spikes.

By the roadside, and in wet meadows, during the late summer or even early in the fall, we find the pink clusters of the false dragonhead.

These blossoms are likely to arouse the suspicion that the plant is related to the turtlehead, but the square stem and four-lobed ovary soon persuade us of its kinship with the members of the Mint Family.

FALSE DRAGONHEAD
Physostegia virginiana

BOUNCING BET. SOAPWORT.

Saponaria officinalis. Pink Family.

Stem. — Rather stout; swollen at the joints. *Leaves.* — Oval; opposite. *Flowers.* — Pink or white; clustered.

A cheery pretty plant is this with large, rose-tinged flowers which are especially effective when double.

Bouncing Bet is of a sociable turn and is seldom found far from civilization, delighting in the proximity of farm-houses and their belongings, in the shape of children, chickens, and cattle. She comes to us from England, and her "feminine comeliness and bounce" suggest to Mr. Burroughs a Yorkshire housemaid. The generic name is from *sapo* — soap — and refers to the lather which the juice forms with water, and which is said to have been used as a substitute for soap.

BOUNCING BET
Saponaria officinalis

IV

RED

Fruit

WILD COLUMBINE *Aquilegia canadensis*

WILD COLUMBINE.

Aquilegia canadensis. Buttercup Family.

Twelve to eighteen inches high. *Stems.* — Branching. *Leaves.* — Much-divided; the leaflets lobed. *Flowers.* — Large; bright red; yellow within; nodding.

> "— A woodland walk,
> A quest of river-grapes, a mocking thrush,
> A wild-rose or rock-loving columbine,
> Salve my worst wounds,"

declares Emerson; and while perhaps few among us are able to make so light-hearted and sweeping a claim for ourselves, yet many will admit the soothing power of which the woods and fields know the secret, and will own that the ordinary annoyances of life may be held more or less in abeyance by one who lives in close sympathy with nature.

About the columbine there is a daring loveliness which stamps it on the memories of even those who are not ordinarily minute observers. It contrives to secure a foothold in the most precipitous and uncertain of nooks, its jewel-like flowers gleaming from their lofty perches with a graceful *insouciance* which awakens our sportsmanlike instincts and fires us with the ambition to equal it in daring and make its loveliness our own. Perhaps it is as well if our greediness be foiled and we get a tumble for our pains, for no flower loses more with its surroundings than the columbine. Indeed, these destructive tendencies, which are strong within most of us, generally defeat themselves by decreasing our pleasure in a blossom the moment we have ruthlessly and without purpose snatched it from its environment. If we honestly wish to study its structure, or to bring into our homes for preservation a bit of the woods' loveliness, its interest and beauty are sure to repay us. But how many pluck every striking flower they see only to toss it carelessly aside when they reach their destination, if they have not already dropped it by the way. Surely if in such small matters sense and self-control were inculcated in children, more would grow up to the poet's standard of worthiness:

"Hast thou named all the birds without a gun?
Loved the wood-rose and left it on its stalk?
At rich men's tables eaten bread and pulse?
Unarmed, faced danger with a heart of trust?
And loved so well a high behavior,
In man or maid, that thou from speech refrained,
Nobility more nobly to repay?
O, be my friend, and teach me to be thine!"*

The name of columbine is derived from *columba* — a dove, but its significance is disputed. Some believe that it was associated with the bird-like claws of the blossom; while Dr. Prior maintains that it refers to the "resemblance of its nectaries to the heads of pigeons in a ring around a dish, a favorite device of ancient artists."

The meaning of the generic title is also doubtful. Gray derived it from *aquilegus* — water-drawing, but gave no further explanation, while other writers claim that it is from *aquila,* an eagle, seeing a likeness to the talons of an eagle in the curved nectaries.

RED TRILLIUM. WAKEROBIN. BIRTHROOT.

Trillium erectum. Lily Family.

Stem. — Stout; from a tuber-like rootstock. *Leaves.* — Broadly ovate; three in a whorl a short distance below the flower. *Flower.* — Single; terminal; usually purplish red, occasionally whitish, pinkish, or greenish; on an erect or somewhat inclined flower-stalk. *Fruit.* — A large, ovate, six-angled reddish berry.

This wakerobin is one of the few self-assertive flowers of the early year. Its contemporaries act as if somewhat uncertain as to whether the spring had really come to stay, but no such lack of confidence possesses our brilliant young friend, who almost flaunts her lurid petals in our faces, as if to force upon us the welcome news that the time of birds and flowers is at hand. Pretty and

---

*Emerson.

suggestive as is the common name, it is hardly appropriate, as the robins have been on the alert for many days before our flower unfurls its crimson signal. Its odor is most unpleasant. Its reddish fruit is noticeable in the woods of late summer.

The sessile trillium, *T. sessile,* has no separate flower-stalk, its red or greenish blossom being set close to the stem leaves. Its petals are narrower, and its leaves are often blotched or spotted. Its berry is globular, six-angled, and red or purplish.

The wakerobins are native to North America, only one species being found just beyond the boundaries in the Russian territory.

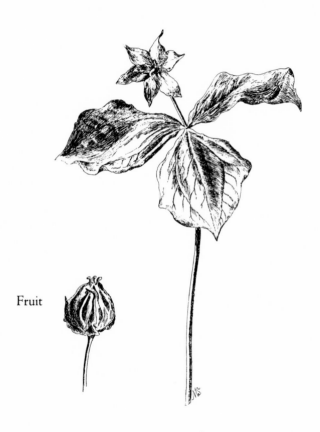

Fruit

RED TRILLIUM *Trillium erectum*

PAINTED-CUP. INDIAN PAINTBRUSH.

Castilleja coccinea. Snapdragon Family.

Stem. — Hairy; six inches to a foot high. *Root-leaves.* — Clustered; oblong. *Stem-leaves.* — Incised; those among the flowers three to five-cleft, bright scarlet toward the summit; showy. *Flowers.* — Pale yellow; spiked.

> "— Scarlet tufts
> Are glowing in the green like flakes of fire;
> The wanderers of the prairie know them well,
> And call that brilliant flower the painted cup."*

But we need not go to the prairie in order to see this plant, for it is equally abundant in certain low sandy New England meadows as well as in the near vicinity of New York City. Under date of June 3d, Thoreau graphically describes its appearance near Concord, Mass.: "The painted cup is in its prime. It reddens the meadow, painted-cup meadow. It is a splendid show of brilliant scarlet, the color of the cardinal flower, and surpassing it in mass and profusion. . . . I do not like the name. It does not remind me of a cup, rather of a flame when it first appears. It might be called flame-flower, or scarlet tip. Here is a large meadow full of it, and yet very few in the town have ever seen it. It is startling to see a leaf thus brilliantly painted, as if its tip were dipped into some scarlet tincture, surpassing most flowers in intensity of color."

TURK'S-CAP LILY.

Lilium superbum. Lily Family.

Stem. — Three to seven feet high. *Leaves.* — Lance-shaped; the lower whorled. *Flowers.* — Orange or scarlet, with purple spots within; three inches long; from three to forty growing in pyramidal clusters.

---

*Bryant.

PAINTED-CUP
Castilleja coccinea

Single flower

TURK'S-CAP LILY
Lilium superbum

"Consider the lilies of the field, how they grow;
    They toil not, neither do they spin;
    And yet I say unto you, that even Solomon in all his glory
    Was not arrayed like one of these."

How they come back to us, the beautiful hackneyed lines, and flash into our memories with new significance of meaning when we chance suddenly upon a meadow bordered with these the most gorgeous of our wild flowers.

We might doubt whether our native lilies at all resembled those alluded to in the scriptural passage, if we did not know that a nearly allied species grew abundantly in Palestine; for we have reason to believe that *lily* was a title freely applied by many Oriental poets to any beautiful flower.

Perhaps this plant never attains far inland the same luxuriance of growth which is common to it in some of the New England lowlands near the coast. Its radiant, nodding blossoms are seen in great profusion as we travel by rail from New York to Boston.

Ironweed
Vernonia noveboracensis
(page 255)

Turk's-Cap Lily
Lilium superbum
(page 212)

Bee-Balm
Monarda didyma
(page 221)

Water-Hemlock
Cicuta maculata
(page 69)

Black-eyed Susan
Rudbeckia hirta
(page 125)

Sundrop
Oenothera fruticosa
(page 122)

Virginia Meadow-Beauty
Rhexia virginica
(page 189)

Blue-eyed Grass
Sisyrinchium angustifolium
(page 228)

Hop Clover
Trifolium agrarium
(page 114)

PASTURES

WOOD LILY. WILD RED LILY.

Lilium philadelphicum. Lily Family.

Stem. — Two to three feet high. *Leaves.* — Whorled or scattered; narrowly lance-shaped. *Flower.* — Erect; orange-red or scarlet, spotted with purple.

Here and there in the shadowy woods is a vivid dash of color made by some wild red lily which has caught a stray sunbeam in its glowing cup. The purple spots on its sepals guide the greedy bee to the nectar at their base; we too can take the hint and reap a

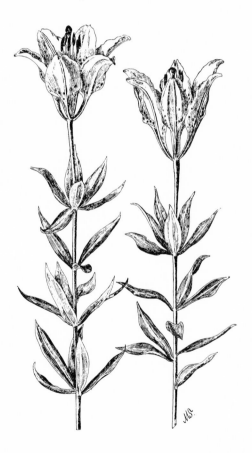

WOOD LILY *Lilium philadelphicum*

sweet reward if we will, after which we are more in sympathy with those eager, humming bees.

This erect, deep-hued flower is so different from its nodding sister of the meadows, that we wonder that the two should be so often confused. When seen away from its surroundings it has less charms perhaps than either the yellow or the Turk's-cap lily; but when it rears itself in the cool depths of its woodland home we feel the uniqueness of its beauty.

BUTTERFLY-WEED. PLEURISY-ROOT.

Asclepias tuberosa. Milkweed Family.

Stem. — Rough and hairy; one to two feet high; erect; very leafy, branching at the summit; without milky juice. *Leaves.* — Linear to narrowly lance-shaped. *Flowers.* — Bright orange-red; in flat-topped, terminal clusters, otherwise closely resembling those of the common milkweed. *Fruit.* — Two hoary erect pods, one of them often stunted.

Few if any of our native plants add more to the beauty of the midsummer landscape than the milkweeds, and of this family no member is more satisfying to the color-craving eye than the gorgeous butterfly-weed, whose vivid flower clusters flame from the dry sandy meadows with such luxuriance of growth as to seem almost tropical. Even in the tropics one hardly sees anything more brilliant than the great masses of color made by these flowers along some of our New England railways in July, while farther south they are said to grow even more profusely. Its gay coloring has given the plant its name of butterfly-weed,* while that of pleurisy-root arose from the belief that the thick, deep root was a remedy for pleurisy. The Indians used it as food and prepared a crude sugar from the flowers; the young seed-pods they boiled and ate with

---

*It is believed by some that the name springs from the fact that butterflies visit the plant.

buffalo-meat. The plant is worthy of cultivation and is easily trans-
planted, as the fleshy roots when broken in pieces form new plants.
Oddly enough, at the Centennial Exhibition much attention was
attracted by a bed of these beautiful plants which were brought
from Holland. Truly, flowers, like prophets, are not without honor
save in their own country.

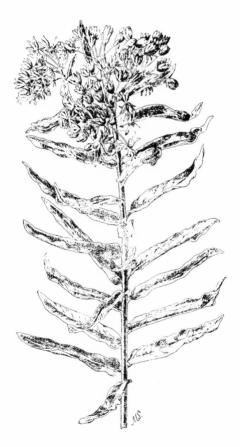

BUTTERFLY-WEED *Asclepias tuberosa*

PITCHER-PLANT. SIDESADDLE-FLOWER. HUNTSMAN'S-CUP.

Sarracenia purpurea. Pitcher-plant Family.

Scape. — Naked; one-flowered; about one foot high. *Leaves.* — Pitcher-shaped; broadly winged; hooded. *Flower.* — Red, pink, or greenish; large; nodding.

The first finding of even the leaves of the pitcher-plant is not to be forgotten. For the leaves not only attract attention by their occasional rich markings, and by their odd pitcher-like shape, but they arouse curiosity by the trap which they set for unwary insects. They are partly lined with a sugary exudation, below which, for a space, they are highly polished, while still lower grow stiff, down-pointing bristles. Insects attracted by the sweet secretion soon find themselves prisoners, as they can seldom fight their way upward through the opposing bristles, or escape by a flight so perpendicular as would be necessary from the form of the cavity. It is rarely that one finds a plant whose leaves are not partially filled with water and drowned insects, and these latter are believed to contribute to its nourishment. In an entry in his journal one September, Thoreau writes of a certain swamp:

"Though the moss is comparatively dry, I cannot walk without upsetting the numerous pitchers, which are now full of water, and so wetting my feet;" and continues: "I once accidentally sat down on such a bed of pitcher plants, and found an uncommonly wet seat where I expected a dry one. These leaves are of various colors, from plain green to a rich striped yellow or deep red. Old Josselyn called this 'hollow-leaved lavender.' I think we have no other plant so singular and remarkable." And November 15th he finds "the water frozen solid in the leaves of the pitcher plant." But singular and interesting though these leaves are, the greatest charm of the plant, it seems to me, lies in its beautiful and unusual flower. This flower we find, if we have the luck, during the early part of June. Although I believe its most frequent color is red (Thoreau likens it to "a great dull red rose," but Gray accuses it of being "deep purple"), I have usually found it either pink or green — fresh delicate shades of both colors — and with a fragrance suggesting sandalwood.

And though (unlike some fortunate friends) I have never found these blossoms rearing themselves by the hundred in an open swamp, baring their beauty to the sunlight, it will be long before I forget the throb of delight which followed my first sight of the plant in a shaded bog, where its delicately tinted flowers nodded almost undetected under bending ferns and masses of false hellebore.

PITCHER-PLANT
Sarracenia purpurea

BEE-BALM. OSWEGO-TEA.

Monarda didyma. Mint Family.

Stem. — Square; erect; about two feet high. *Leaves.* — Opposite; ovate, pointed; aromatic; those near the flowers tinged with red. *Flowers.* — Bright red; clustered in a close round head.

We have so few red flowers that when one flashes suddenly upon us it gives us a pleasant thrill of wonder and surprise. The red flowers know so well how to enhance their beauty by seeking an appropriate setting. They select the rich green backgrounds only found in moist, shady places, and are peculiarly charming when associated with a lonely marsh or a mountain-brook. The bee-balm especially haunts these cool nooks, and its rounded flower-clusters touch with warmth the shadows of the damp woods of midsummer. The Indians named the flower *O-gee-chee* — flaming flower, and are said to have made a tea-like decoction from the blossoms.

CARDINAL-FLOWER
Lobelia cardinalis

BEE-BALM
Monarda didyma

Single flower

CARDINAL-FLOWER.

Lobelia cardinalis. Bluebell Family.

Stem. — From two to four feet high. *Leaves.* — Alternate; narrowly oblong; slightly toothed. *Flowers.* — Bright red; growing in a raceme.

We have no flower which can vie with this in vivid coloring. In late summer its brilliant red gleams from the marshes or is reflected from the shadowy water's edge with unequalled intensity —

> "As if some wounded eagle's breast
> Slow throbbing o'er the plain,
> Had left its airy path impressed
> In drops of scarlet rain."*

The early French Canadians were so struck with its beauty that they sent the plant to France as a specimen of what the wilds of the New World could yield. Perhaps at that time it received its English name which likens it to the gorgeously attired dignitaries of the Roman Church.

TRUMPET HONEYSUCKLE.

Lonicera sempervirens. Honeysuckle Family.

A twining shrub. *Leaves.* — Entire; opposite; oblong; the upper pairs united around the stem. *Flowers.* — Deep red without, yellowish within; in close clusters from the axils of the upper leaves. *Fruit.* — A red or orange berry.

Many of us are so familiar with these flowers in our gardens that we have, perhaps, considered them "escapes" when we found them brightening the pasture thicket where really they are most at home, appearing at any time from May till October.

---

*Oliver Wendell Holmes.

SCARLET PIMPERNEL. POOR MAN'S WEATHERGLASS.

Anagallis arvensis. Primrose Family.

Stems. — Low; spreading. *Leaves.* — Opposite; ovate; set close to the stem; usually with dark spots. *Flowers.* — Bright red, occasionally blue or white; growing singly from the axils of the leaves.

This flower is found in clefts of rocks or in sandy fields, and is noted for its sensitiveness to the weather. It folds its petals at the approach of rain and fails to open at all on a wet or cloudy day. Even in fine weather it closes in the early afternoon and "sleeps" till the next morning. Its ripened seeds are of value as food for many song-birds. It was thought at one time to be serviceable in liver complaints, which reputed virtue may have given rise to the old couplet:

> "No ear hath heard, no tongue can tell
> The virtues of the pimpernell."

SCARLET PIMPERNEL *Anagallis arvensis*

V

BLUE AND PURPLE

BLUETS
Houstonia caerulea

ROUND-LOBED
HEPATICA
Hepatica americana

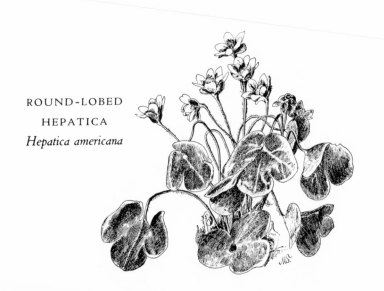

BLUETS. QUAKER-LADIES.

Houstonia caerulea. Bedstraw Family.

Stem. — Erect; three to five inches high. *Leaves.* — Very small; opposite. *Flowers.* — Small; delicate blue, lilac, or nearly white, with a yellowish eye.

No one who has been in New England during the month of May can forget the loveliness of the bluets. The roadsides, meadows, and even the lawns are thickly carpeted with the dainty enamel-like blossoms, which are always pretty, but which seem to flourish with especial vigor and in great profusion in this lovely region. Less plentiful, perhaps, but still common is the little plant in grassy places far south and west, blossoming in early spring.

The flowers are among those which botanists term "dimorphous." This word signifies *occurring in two forms,* and refers to the stamens and pistils, which vary in size, some flowers having a tall pistil and short stamens, others tall stamens and a short pistil. Darwin has proved, not only that one of these flowers can seldom fully fertilize itself, but that usually the blossoms with tall pistils must be fertilized with pollen from the tall stamens, and that the short pistils are only acted upon by the short stamens. With a good magnifier and a needle these two forms can easily be studied. This is one of the many interesting safeguards against close fertilization.

ROUND-LOBED HEPATICA. LIVERLEAF.

Hepatica americana. Buttercup Family.

Scape. — Fuzzy; one-flowered. *Leaves.* — Rounded; three-lobed; from the root. *Flowers.* — Blue, white, or pinkish.

> "The liver-leaf puts forth her sister blooms
> Of faintest blue —"

soon after the late snows have melted. Indeed these fragile-looking, enamel-like flowers are sometimes found actually beneath the snow, and form one of the many instances which we encounter among flowers, as among their human contemporaries, where the frail and delicate-looking withstand storm and stress far better than their more robust-appearing brethren. We welcome these tiny newcomers with especial joy, not alone for their delicate beauty, but because they are usually the first of all the flowers upon the scene of action, if we rule out the never-tardy skunk-cabbage. The rusty leaves of last summer are obliged to suffice for the plant's foliage until some little time after the blossoms have appeared, when the young fresh leaves begin to uncurl themselves. Someone has suggested that the fuzzy little buds look as though they were still wearing their furs as a protection against the wintry weather which so often stretches late into our spring. The flowers vary in color from a lovely blue to pink or white. They are found chiefly in the woods, but occasionally on the sunny hill-sides as well.

The generic name, *Hepatica*, is from the Greek for liver, and was probably given to the plant on account of the shape of its leaf. Dr. Prior says that "in consequence of this fancied likeness it was used as a remedy for liver-complaints, the common people having long labored under the belief that Nature indicated in some such fashion the uses to which her creations might be applied."

BLUE-EYED GRASS.

Sisyrinchium angustifolium. Iris Family.

Four to twelve inches high. *Leaves.* — Narrow and grass-like. *Flowers.* — Blue or purple, with a yellow centre.

> "For the sun is no sooner risen with a burning heat,
>   But it withereth the grass,
>   And the flower thereof falleth,
>   And the grace of the fashion of it perisheth."

So reads the passage in the Epistle of St. James, which seems so graphically to describe the brief life of this little flower that we might almost believe the Apostle had had it in mind, were it to be found in the East.

The blue-eyed grass belongs to the same family as the showy

fleur-de-lis, and blossoms during the summer, being especially plentiful in moist meadows. It is sometimes called "eyebright," which name belongs by rights to *Euphrasia americana*.

GILL-OVER-THE-GROUND. GROUND-IVY.

Glechoma hederacea. Mint Family.

Stems. — Creeping and trailing. *Leaves.* — Small and kidney-shaped. *Flowers.* — Bluish-purple; loosely clustered in the axils of the leaves.

As the pleasant aroma of its leaves suggests, this little plant is closely allied to the catnip. Its common title of Gill-over-the-

GILL-OVER-THE-GROUND
Glechoma hederacea

BLUE-EYED GRASS
Sisyrinchium angustifolium

ground appeals to one who is sufficiently without interest in pasture-land (for it is obnoxious to cattle) to appreciate the pleasant fashion in which this little immigrant from Europe has made itself at home here, brightening the earth with such a generous profusion of blossoms every May. But it is somewhat of a disappointment to learn that this name is derived from the French *guiller,* and refers to its former use in the fermentation of beer. Oddly enough the name of alehoof, which the plant has borne in England and which naturally has been supposed to refer to this same custom, is said by a competent authority (Professor Earle, of Oxford*) to have no connection with it, but to signify *another sort of hofe, hofe* being the early English name for the violet, which resembles these flowers in color.

The plant was highly prized formerly as a domestic medicine. Gerard claims that "boiled in mutton-broth it helpeth weake and akeing backs."

---

*John Earle, professor of Anglo-Saxon from 1848 to 1903.

Wild Cucumber
Echinocystis lobata
(page 74)

Virgin's-Bower
Clematis virginiana
(page 76)

Nightshade
Solanum dulcamara
(page 250)

Wild Morning-Glory
Convolvulus sepium
(page 188)

Groundnut
Apios americana
(page 274)

Hog-Peanut
Amphicarpa bracteata
(page 261)

Common Dodder
Cuscuta gronovii
(page 77)

Climbing False Buckwheat
Polygonum scandens
(page 79)

VINES

WILD GERANIUM. WILD CRANESBILL.

Geranium maculatum. Geranium Family.

Stem. — Erect; hairy. *Leaves.* — About five-parted, the divisions lobed and cut. *Flowers.* — Pale pink-purple; rather large.

In spring and early summer the open woods and shaded road-sides are abundantly brightened with these graceful flowers. They are of peculiar interest because of their close kinship with the species, *G. pratense,* which first attracted the attention of the German scholar, Sprengel,* to the close relations existing between flowers and insects. The beak-like appearance of its fruit gives the plant both its popular and scientific names, for *geranium* is from the Greek for crane. The specific title, *maculatum,* refers to the somewhat blotched appearance of the older leaves.

---

*Christian Konrad Sprengel, a botanist (1750–1816).

WILD GERANIUM

Geranium maculatum

LARGER BLUE FLAG. FLEUR-DE-LIS.

Iris versicolor. Iris Family.

Stem. — Stout; angled on one side; leafy; one to three feet high.
Leaves. — Flat and sword-shaped, with their inner surfaces coherent for
about half of their length. *Flowers.* — Large and showy; violet-blue, var-
iegated with green, yellow, or white; purple-veined.

> "Born in the purple, born to joy and pleasance,
>   Thou dost not toil nor spin,
> But makest glad and radiant with thy presence
>   The meadow and the lin."*

In both form and color this is one of the most regal of our wild
flowers, and it is easy to understand why the fleur-de-lis was chosen
as the emblem of a royal house, although the especial flower which
Louis VII of France selected as his badge was probably white.

It will surprise most of us to learn that the common name which
we have borrowed from the French does not signify "flower-of-the-
lily," as it would if literally translated, but "flower of Louis," *lis*
being a corruption of the name of the king who first adopted it as
his badge.

For the botanist the blue flag possesses special interest. It is a
conspicuous example of a flower which has guarded itself against
self-fertilization, and which is beautifully calculated to secure the
opposite result. The position of the stamens is such that their pollen could not easily reach the stigmas of the same flower, for these
are borne on the inner surface of the petal-like, overarching styles.
There is no prospect here of any seed being set unless the pollen
of another flower is secured. Now what are the chances in favor
of this? They are many: In the first place the blossom is unusually
large and showy, from its size and shape alone almost certain to
arrest the attention of the passing bee; next, the color is not only
conspicuous, but it is also one which has been found to be especially
attractive to bees, blue and purple flowers being particularly sought
by these insects. When the bee reaches the flower he alights on

---

*Longfellow.

234

the only convenient landing-place, one of the recurved sepals; following the deep purple veins which experience has taught him lead to the hidden nectar, he thrusts his head below the anther, brushing off its pollen, which he carries to another flower.

The rootstocks of the Florentine species of iris yield the familiar "orris-root."

The family name is from the Greek for *rainbow,* on account of the rich and varied hues of its different members.

The plant abounds in wet meadows, the blossoms appearing in June.

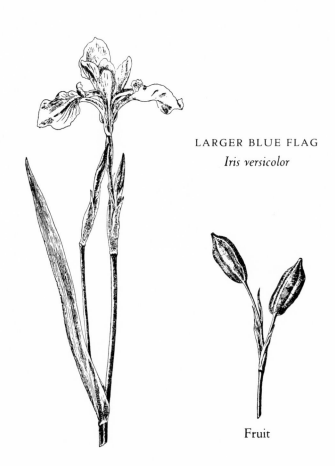

LARGER BLUE FLAG
Iris versicolor

Fruit

AMERICAN BROOKLIME.

Veronica americana. Snapdragon Family.

Stem. — Smooth; reclining at base, then erect; eight to fifteen inches high. *Leaves.* — Mostly opposite; oblong; toothed. *Flowers.* — Blue; clustered in the axils of the leaves.

Perhaps the prettiest of the blue *Veronicas* is the American brooklime. Its clustered flowers make bright patches in moist ground which might, at a little distance, be mistaken for beds of forget-me-nots. It blossoms from June till August, and is almost as common in wet ditches and meadows as its sister, the common speedwell, is in dry and open places. Some of the members of this genus were once believed to possess great medicinal virtues, and won for themselves in Europe the laudatory names of Honor and Praise.

SKULLCAP.

Scutellaria. Mint Family.

Stem. — Square; usually one to two feet high. *Leaves.* — Opposite; oblong; lance-shaped or linear. *Flowers.* — Blue.

The prettiest and most striking of this genus is the hyssop skull-cap, *S. integrifolia,* whose bright blue flowers are about one inch long, growing in terminal racemes. In June and July they may be found among the long grass of the roadsides and meadows. They are easily identified by the curious little appendage on the upper part of the calyx, which gives to this genus its common name.

Perhaps the best-known member of the group is the mad-dog skullcap, *S. lateriflora,* which delights in wet places, bearing small, inconspicuous flowers in one-sided racemes. This plant is quite smooth, while that of *S. integrifolia* is rather downy. It was formerly believed to be a sure cure for hydrophobia.

The flowers of the common skullcap, *S. epilobiifolia,* are much larger than those of *S. lateriflora,* but smaller than those of *S. integrifolia.* They grow singly from the axils of the upper leaves.

AMERICAN BROOKLIME
Veronica americana

Flower

COMMON SKULLCAP
Scutellaria epilobiifolia

COMMON BLUE VIOLET.

Viola papilionacea. Violet Family.

Scape. — Slender; one-flowered. *Leaves.* — Heart-shaped, all from the root. *Flowers.* — Varying from a pale blue to deep purple, borne singly on a scape.

Perhaps this is the best-beloved as well as the best-known of the early wild flowers. Whose heart has not been gladdened at one time or another by a glimpse of some fresh green nook in early May where

> "— purple violets lurk,
> With all the lovely children of the shade?"

It seems as if no other flower were so suggestive of the dawning year, so associated with the days when life was full of promise. Although I believe that more than a hundred species of violets have been recorded, only about thirty are found in our country; of these perhaps twenty are native to the Northeastern States. Unfortunately we have no strongly sweet-scented species, none

> "— sweeter than the lids of Juno's eyes
> Or Cytherea's breath, —"

as Shakespeare found the English blossom. Prophets and warriors as well as poets have favored the violet; Mahomet preferred it to

Witch Hazel
Hamamelis virginiana
(page 145)

Sweet Pepperbush
Clethra alnifolia

Chicory
Cichorium intybus
(page 257)

Stiff Gentian
Gentiana quinquefolia
(page 264)

Closed Gentian
Gentiana andrewsii
(page 264)

Fringed Gentian
Gentiana crinita
(page 262)

FALL

all other flowers, and it was chosen by the Bonapartes as their emblem.

Perhaps its frequent mention by ancient writers is explained by the discovery that the name was once applied somewhat indiscriminately to sweet-scented blossoms.

The birdfoot violet, *V. pedata,* unlike other members of the family, has leaves which are divided into linear lobes. Its flower is peculiarly lovely, being large and velvety. The variety *bicolor* is especially striking and pansy-like, its two upper petals being of a deeper hue than the others. It is found in the neighborhood of Washington in abundance, and on the shaly soil of New Jersey.

An interesting feature of many of these plants is their cleistogamous flowers. These are small and inconspicuous blossoms, which never open (thus guarding their pollen against all depredations), but which are self-fertilized, ripening their seeds in the dark. They are usually found near or beneath the ground, and are often taken for immature buds.

PURPLE FRINGED ORCHISES.
Orchid Family.

Habenaria fimbriata.

Leaves. — Oval or oblong; the upper, few, passing into lance-shaped bracts. *Flowers.* — Purple; rather large; with a fan-shaped, three-parted lip, its divisions fringed; with a long curving spur; growing in a spike.

Habenaria psycodes.

Leaves. — Oblong or lance-shaped; the upper passing into linear bracts. *Flowers.* — Purple; fragrant; resembling those of *H. fimbriata,* but much smaller, with a less fringed lip; growing in a spike.

We should search the wet meadows in early June if we wish surely to be in time for the larger of the purple fringed orchises, for *H. fimbriata* somewhat antedates *H. psycodes,* which is the commoner species of the two and appears in July. Under date of June

9th, Thoreau writes: "Find the great fringed-orchis out apparently two or three days, two are almost fully out, two or three only budded; a large spike of peculiarly delicate, pale-purple flowers growing in the luxuriant and shady swamp, amid hellebores, ferns, golden senecio, etc. . . . The village belle never sees this more delicate belle of the swamp. . . . A beauty reared in the shade of a convent, who has never strayed beyond the convent-bell. Only the skunk or owl, or other inhabitant of the swamp, beholds it."

MONKEY-FLOWER.

Mimulus ringens. Snapdragon Family.

Stem. — Square; one to two feet high. *Leaves.* — Opposite; oblong or lance-shaped. *Flowers.* — Pale violet-purple, rarely white; growing singly from the axils of the leaves.

From July onward the monkey-flowers tinge the wet fields and border the streams and ponds; not growing in the water like the pickerelweed, but seeking a hummock in the swamp, or a safe foothold on the brook's edge, where they can absorb the moisture requisite to their vigorous growth.

The name is a diminutive of *mimus* — a buffoon, and refers to the somewhat grinning blossom. The plant is a common one throughout the eastern part of the country.

BLUE VERVAIN. SIMPLER'S-JOY.

Verbena hastata. Vervain Family.

Four to six feet high. *Leaves.* — Opposite; somewhat lance-shaped; the lower often lobed and sometimes halberd-shaped at base. *Flowers.* — Purple; small; in slender erect spikes.

Along the roadsides in midsummer we notice these slender purple spikes, the appearance of which would be vastly improved if the tiny blossoms would only consent to open simultaneously.

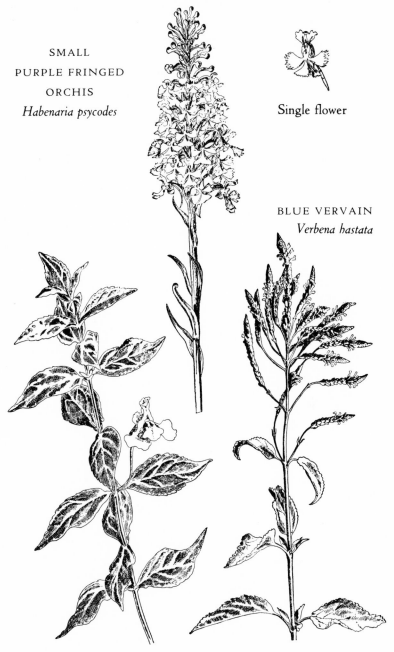

SMALL
PURPLE FRINGED
ORCHIS
Habenaria psycodes

Single flower

BLUE VERVAIN
Verbena hastata

MONKEY-FLOWER *Mimulus ringens*

In earlier times the vervain was beset with classic associations. It was claimed as the plant which Virgil and other poets mention as being used for altar-decorations and for the garlands of sacrificial beasts. It was believed to be the *herba sacra* of the ancients, until it was understood that the generic title *Verbena* was a word which was applied to branches of any description which were used in religious rites. It certainly seems, however, to have been applied to some special plant in the time of Pliny, for he writes that no plant was more honored among the Romans than the sacred *Verbena*. In more modern times as well the vervain has been regarded as an "herb of grace," and has been gathered with various ceremonies and with the invocation of a blessing, which began as follows:

"Hallowed be thou, Vervain,
As thou growest on the ground,
For in the Mount of Calvary
There thou was first found."

It was then supposed to be endued with special virtue, and was worn on the person to avert disaster.

The time-honored title of simpler's-joy arose from the remuneration which this popular plant brought to the "simplers" — as the gatherers of medicinal herbs were entitled.

INDIAN-TOBACCO.

Lobelia inflata. Bluebell Family.

One to two feet high. *Stem.* — Branching from the root. *Leaves.* — Ovate or oblong; somewhat toothed. *Flowers.* — Blue or purple; growing in a long raceme.

During the summer we note in the dry, open fields the blue racemes of the Indian-tobacco, and in the later year the inflated pods which give it its specific name. The plant is said to be poisonous if taken internally, and yields a "quack-medicine" of some notoriety. The Indians smoked its dried leaves, which impart to the tongue a peculiar tobacco-like sensation.

PICKERELWEED.

Pontederia cordata. Pickerelweed Family.

Stem. — Stout; usually one-leaved. *Leaves.* — Arrow or heart-shaped.
Flowers. — Blue; fading quickly; with an unpleasant odor; growing in a
dense spike.

The pickerelweed grows in such shallow water as the pickerel
seek, or else in moist, wet places along the shores of streams and
rivers. We can look for the blue, closely spiked flowers from late
July until some time in September. They are often found near the
delicate arrowhead.

PICKERELWEED
Pontederia cordata

INDIAN-TOBACCO
Lobelia inflata

SELFHEAL. HEAL-ALL.

Prunella vulgaris. Mint Family.

Stems. — Low. *Leaves.* — Opposite; oblong. *Flowers.* — Bluish-purple; in a spike or head.

Throughout the length and breadth of the country, from June until September, the short, close spikes of the selfheal can be found along the roadsides. The botanical name, *Prunella,* is taken from the German for quinsy, for which this plant was considered a certain cure. It was also used in England as an application to the wounds received by rustic laborers, as its common names, carpenter's herb, hook-heal, and sicklewort, imply. That the French had a similar practice is proved by an old proverb of theirs to the effect that "No one wants a surgeon who keeps *Prunelle.*"

SELFHEAL
Prunella vulgaris

SEA-LAVENDER. MARSH-ROSEMARY.

Limonium nashii. Sea-lavender Family.

Stems. — Leafless; branching. *Leaves.* — From the root; somewhat oblong; thick. *Flowers.* — Lavender color or pale purple; tiny; scattered or loosely spiked along one side of the branches.

In August many of the salt marshes are blue with the tiny flowers of the sea-lavender. The spray-like appearance of the little plant would seem to account for its name of rosemary, which is derived from the Latin for *sea-spray,* but Dr. Prior states that this name was given it on account of "its usually growing on the sea-coast, and its odor."

Blossoming with the lavender we often find the great rose-mallows and the dainty sea-pinks. The marsh St. Johnswort as well is frequently a neighbor, and, a little later in the season, the salt-marsh fleabane.

SEA-LAVENDER
Limonium nashii

VIPER'S BUGLOSS. BLUEWEED.

Echium vulgare. Forget-me-not Family.

Stem. — Rough; bristly; erect; about two feet high. *Leaves.* — Alternate; lance-shaped; set close to the stem. *Flowers.* — Bright blue; spiked on one side of the branches, which are at first rolled up from the end, straightening as the blossoms expand.

When the blueweed first came to us from across the sea it secured a foothold in Virginia. Since then it has gradually worked its way northward, lining the Hudson's shores, overrunning many of the dry fields in its vicinity, and making itself at home in parts of New England. We should be obliged to rank it among the "pesti-

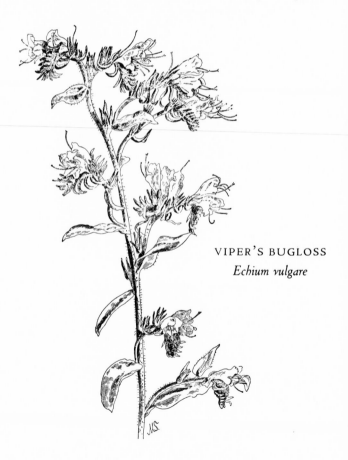

VIPER'S BUGLOSS
Echium vulgare

ferous" weeds were it not that, as a rule, it only seeks to monopolize land which is not good for very much else. The pinkish buds and bright blue blossoms, with their red protruding stamens, make a valuable addition, from the aesthetic point of view, to the bunch of midsummer field-flowers in which hitherto the various shades of red and yellow have predominated.

BEACH PEA
Lathyrus japonicus

BEACH PEA.

Lathyrus japonicus. Pea Family.

About one foot high, or more. *Stem.* — Stout. *Leaves.* — Divided into from three to five pairs of thick oblong leaflets. *Flowers.* — Large; purple; clustered.

The deep-hued flowers of this stout plant are commonly found along the sand-hills of the seashore, and also on the shores of the Great Lakes, blooming in early summer. Both flowers and leaves are at once recognized as belonging to the Pea family.

NIGHTSHADE.

Solanum dulcamara. Tomato Family.

Stem. — Usually somewhat climbing or twining. *Leaves.* — Heart-shaped; the upper halberd-shaped or with ear-like lobes or leaflets at the base. *Flowers.* — Purple; in small clusters. *Fruit.* — A red berry.

The purple flowers, which at once betray their kinship with the potato plant, and, in late summer, the bright red berries of the nightshade, cluster about the fences and clamber over the moist banks which line the highway. This plant, which was imported from Europe, usually indicates the presence of civilization. It is not poi-

NIGHTSHADE
Solanum dulcamara

Fruit

sonous to the touch, as is often supposed, and it is doubtful if the berries have the baneful power attributed to them. Thoreau writes regarding them: "The Solanum Dulcamara berries are another kind which grow in drooping clusters. I do not know any clusters more graceful and beautiful than these drooping cymes of scented or translucent, cherry-colored elliptical berries. . . . They hang more gracefully over the river's brim than any pendant in a lady's ear. Yet they are considered poisonous; not to look at surely. . . . But why should they not be poisonous? Would it not be bad taste to eat these berries which are ready to feed another sense?"

BLAZING-STAR.

Liatris spicata. Composite Family.

Stem. — Simple; stout; hoary; two to five feet high. *Leaves.* — Alternate, narrowly lance-shaped. *Flower-heads.* — Racemed along the upper part of the stem; composed entirely of tubular flowers of a beautiful shade of rose-purple.

BLAZING-STAR

Liatris spicata

These showy and beautiful flowers lend still another tint to the many-hued salt marshes and glowing inland meadows of the falling year. Gray assigns them to dry localities from New England to Minnesota and southward, while my own experience of them is limited to the New England coast, where their stout leafy stems and bright-hued blossoms are noticeable among the goldenrods and asters of September. The hasty observer sometimes confuses the plant with the ironweed, but the two flowers are very different in color and in their manner of growth.

BLUE AND PURPLE ASTERS.

Aster. Composite Family.

Flower-heads. — Composed of blue or purple ray-flowers, with a centre of yellow disk-flowers.

As about one hundred and twenty different species of aster are native to the United States, and as fifty-four of these are found in Northeastern America, all but a dozen being purple or blue (*i.e.,* with purple or blue ray-flowers), and as even botanists find that it requires patient application to distinguish these many species, only a brief description of the more conspicuous and common ones is here attempted.

The broad-leaved aster, *A. macrophyllus,* is best known, perhaps, by the great colonies of large, rounded, somewhat heart-shaped, long-stemmed leaves with which it carpets the woods long before the flowers appear. Finally it sends up a stout, rigid stalk two to three feet high, bearing smaller oblong leaves and clusters of lavender or violet-colored flower-heads.

Along the dry roadsides in early August we may look for the bright blue-purple flowers of *A. patens.* This is a low-growing species, with rough, narrowly oblong, clasping leaves, and widely spreading branches, whose slender branchlets are usually terminated by a solitary flower-head.

Probably no member of the group is more striking than the New England aster, *A. novae-angliae,* whose stout hairy stem (sometimes eight feet high), numerous lance-shaped leaves, and large violet-

NEW ENGLAND ASTER

Aster novae-angliae

Disk and ray-flower

purple or sometimes pinkish flower-heads, are conspicuous in the swamps of late summer.

A. puniceus is another tall swamp species, with long showy pale lavender ray-flowers.

One of the most commonly encountered asters is *A. cordifolius,* which is far from being the only heart-leaved species, despite its title. Its many small, pale blue or almost white flower-heads mass themselves abundantly along the wood-borders and shaded road-sides.

The New York aster, *A. novi-belgii,* is a slender-stemmed, branching plant, usually from one to three feet high, with lance-shaped leaves and violet flower-heads. It is found in swampy places near the coast from August to October. Gray calls it "the commonest late-flowered aster of the Atlantic border, and variable."

Perhaps the loveliest of all the tribe is the seaside purple aster, *A. spectabilis,* a low plant with narrowly oblong leaves and large bright heads, the violet-purple ray-flowers of which are nearly an inch long. This grows in sandy soil near the coast and may be found putting forth its royal, daisy-like blossoms into November.

This beautiful genus, like that of the goldenrod, is one of the peculiar glories of our country. Every autumn these two kinds of flowers clothe our roadsides and meadows with so regal a mantle of purple and gold that we cannot but wonder if the flowers of any other region combine in such a radiant display.

GREAT LOBELIA.

Lobelia siphilitica. Bluebell Family.

Stem. — Leafy; somewhat hairy; one to three feet high. *Leaves.* — Alternate; ovate to lance-shaped; thin; irregularly toothed. *Flowers.* — Rather large; light blue; spiked.

The great lobelia is a striking plant which grows in low ground, flowering from midsummer into the fall. In some places it is called "High-Belia," a pun which is supposed to reflect upon the less tall and conspicuous species, such as the Indian-tobacco, *L. inflata,* which are found flowering at the same season.

If one of its blossoms is examined, the pistil is seen to be enclosed by the united stamens in such a fashion as to secure self-fertilization, one would suppose. But it is hardly probable that a flower so noticeable as this, and wearing a color as popular as blue, should have adorned itself so lavishly to no purpose. Consequently we are led to inquire more closely into its domestic arrangements. Our curiosity is rewarded by the discovery that the lobes of the stigma are so tightly pressed together that they can at first receive no pollen upon their sensitive surfaces. We also find that the anthers open only by a pore at their tips, and when irritated by the jar of a visiting bee, discharge their pollen upon its body through

GREAT LOBELIA
Lobelia siphilitica

these outlets. This being accomplished the fringed stigma pushes forward, brushing aside whatever pollen may have fallen within the tube. Finally, when it projects beyond the anthers, it opens, and is ready to receive its pollen from the next insect-visitor.

The genus is named after an early Flemish herbalist, de l'Obel.*

IRONWEED.

Vernonia noveboracensis. Composite Family.

Stem. — Leafy; usually tall. *Leaves.* — Alternate; somewhat lance-oblong. *Flower-heads.* — An intense red-purple; loosely clustered; composed entirely of tubular flowers.

---

*Matthias de Lobel (d. 1616).

Along the roadsides and low meadows near the coast the iron-weed adds its deep purple hues to the color-pageant of late August. By the uninitiated the plant is often mistaken for an aster, but a moment's inspection will discover that the minute flowers which compose each flower-head are all tubular in shape, and that the ray or strap-shaped blossoms which an aster must have are wanting. These flower-heads are surrounded by an involucre composed of small scales which are tipped with a tiny point and are usually of a purplish color also.

Flower

IRONWEED *Vernonia noveboracensis*

CHICORY. SUCCORY.

Cichorium intybus. Composite Family.

Stems. — Branching. *Leaves.* — The lower oblong or lance-shaped, partly clasping, sometimes sharply incised; the floral ones minute. *Flower-heads.* — Blue; set close to the stem; composed entirely of strap-shaped flowers; opening at different times.

> "Oh, not in Ladies' gardens,
> My peasant posy!
> Smile thy dear blue eyes,
> Nor only — nearer to the skies —

Single flower

CHICORY *Cichorium intybus*

In upland pastures, dim and sweet, —
But by the dusty road
Where tired feet
Toil to and fro;

Where flaunting Sin
May see thy heavenly hue,
Or weary Sorrow look from thee
Toward a more tender blue."*

This roadside weed blossoms in late summer. It is extensively
cultivated in France, where the leaves are blanched and used in a
salad which is called "Barbe des Capucins." The roots are roasted
and mixed with coffee, both there and in England.

Horace mentions its leaves as part of his frugal fare, and Pliny
remarks upon the importance of the plant to the Egyptians, who
formerly used it in great quantities, and of whose diet it is still a
staple article.

---

*Margaret Deland, an American novelist and poet (1857–1945).

Solomon's-Seal
Polygonatum biflorum
(page 97)

Dutchman's-Breeches
Dicentra cucullaria
(page 14)

Jack-in-the-Pulpit
Arisaema triphyllum
(page 269)

White Baneberry
Actea pachypoda
(page 25)

Squirrel-Corn
Dicentra canadensis
(page 15)

Painted Trillium
Trillium undulatum
(page 17)

Wild Columbine
Aquilegia canadensis
(page 209)

Downy Yellow Violet
Viola pubescens
(page 100)

Wild Ginger
Asarum canadense
(page 272)

Bunchberry
Cornus canadensis
(page 27)

COOL SHADED NOOKS

HOG-PEANUT.

Amphicarpa bracteata. Pea Family.

Stem. — Climbing and twining over plants and shrubs. *Leaves.* — Divided into three somewhat four-sided leaflets. *Flowers.* — Papilionaceous; pale lilac or purplish; in nodding racemes. *Pod.* — One inch long.

Along the shadowy lanes which wind through the woods the climbing members of the Pea family are very abundant. During the late summer and autumn the lonely wayside is skirted by

"Vines, with clust'ring brunches growing;
Plants, with goodly burden bowing."

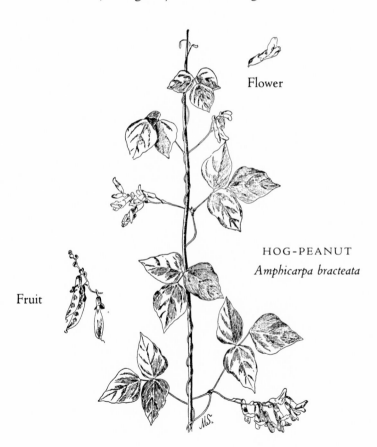

Flower

HOG-PEANUT
Amphicarpa bracteata

Fruit

And in and out among this luxuriant growth twist the slender stems of the ill-named hog-peanut, its delicate lilac blossoms nodding from the coarse stalks of the goldenrods and ironweeds, or blending with the purple asters.

This plant bears flowers of two kinds: the upper ones are perfect, but apparently useless, as they seldom ripen fruit; while the lower or subterranean ones are without petals or attractiveness of appearance, but yield eventually at least one large ripe seed.

FRINGED GENTIAN.

Gentiana crinita. Gentian Family.

Stem. — One to two feet high. *Leaves.* — Opposite, lance-shaped or narrowly oval. *Flowers.* — Blue; large.

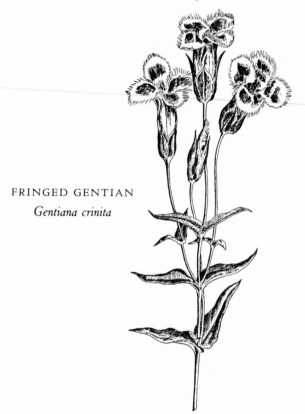

FRINGED GENTIAN
Gentiana crinita

In late September, when we have almost ceased to hope for new flowers, we are in luck if we chance upon this

"— blossom bright with autumn dew,"

whose

"— sweet and quiet eye
Looks through its fringes to the sky,
Blue — blue — as if that sky let fall,
A flower from its cerulean wall;"

for the fringed gentian is fickle in its habits, and the fact that we have located it one season does not mean that we shall find it in the same place the following year; being an annual, with seeds that are easily washed away, it is apt to change its haunts from time to time. So our search for this plant is always attended with the charm of uncertainty. Once having ferreted out its new abiding-place, however, we can satiate ourselves with its loveliness, which it usually lavishes unstintingly upon the moist meadows which it has elected to honor.

Thoreau describes its color as "such a dark blue! surpassing that of the male bluebird's back!" My experience has been that the flowers which grow in the shade are of a clear pure azure, "Heaven's own blue," as Bryant claims; while those which are found in open, sunny meadows may be justly said to vie with the back of the male bluebird. If the season has been a mild one we shall perhaps find a few blossoms lingering into November, but the plant is probably blighted by a severe frost, although Miss Emily Dickinson's little poem voices another opinion:

"But just before the snows
    There came a purple creature
That ravished all the hill:
    And Summer hid her forehead,
    And mockery was still.
The frosts were her condition:
    The Tyrian would not come
Until the North evoked it,
    'Creator! shall I bloom!'"

CLOSED GENTIAN. BOTTLE-GENTIAN.

Gentiana andrewsii. Gentian Family.

Stem. — One to two feet high; upright; smooth. *Leaves.* — Opposite; narrowly oval or lance-shaped. *Flowers.* — Blue to purple; clustered at the summit of the stem and often in the axils of the leaves.

Few flowers adapt themselves better to the season than the closed gentian. We look for it in September when the early waning days and frost-suggestive nights prove so discouraging to the greater part of the floral world. Then in somewhat moist, shaded places along the roadside we find this vigorous, autumnal-looking plant, with stout stems, leaves that bronze as the days advance, and deep-tinted flowers firmly closed as though to protect the delicate reproductive organs within from the sharp touches of the late year.

To me the closed gentian usually shows a deep blue or even purple countenance, although, like the fringed gentian and so many other flowers, its color is lighter in the shade than in the sunlight. But Thoreau claims for it a "transcendent blue," "a splendid blue, light in the shade, turning to purple with age." "Bluer than the bluest sky, they lurk in the moist and shady recesses of the banks," he writes. Mr. Burroughs also finds it "intensely blue."

STIFF GENTIAN. AGUE-WEED.

Gentiana quinquefolia. Gentian Family.

Stem. — Slender; usually branching; one to two feet high. *Leaves.* — Opposite; ovate; lance-shaped; partly clasping. *Flowers.* — Pale blue or purplish; smaller than those of the closed gentian; in clusters of five or more at the summit of stems and branches.

In some localities the stiff gentian is very abundant. Gray assigns the plant to "rich woods" and "damp fields;" I never remember to have encountered it save in more or less mountainous regions. In September it tinges with delicate color the slopes of the Shawangunk mountains and borders the woods and roadsides of the Berkshire hills.

CLOSED GENTIAN
Gentiana andrewsii

STIFF GENTIAN
Gentiana quinquefolia

BLUEBELLS. VIRGINIA COWSLIP. LUNGWORT.

Mertensia virginica. Forget-me-not Family.

One to two feet high. *Stem.* — Smooth; pale, erect. *Leaves.* — Oblong; veiny. *Flowers.* — Blue, pinkish in bud; in raceme-like clusters which are rolled up from the end and straighten as the flowers expand.

These very lovely blossoms are found in moist places during April and May in parts of New York as well as south and westward. The English naturalist, Mr. Alfred Wallace, seeing them, for the first time, in the vicinity of Cincinnati, writes in the *Fortnightly Review*: "In a damp river bottom the exquisite blue *Mertensia Virginica* was found. It is called here the 'Virginian cowslip,' its drooping porcelain-blue bells being somewhat of the size and form of those of the true cowslip."

VI

MISCELLANEOUS

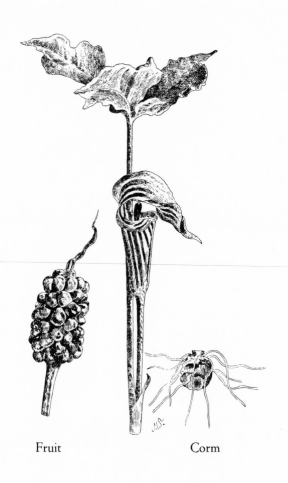

Fruit   Corm

JACK-IN-THE-PULPIT *Arisaema triphyllum*

JACK-IN-THE-PULPIT. INDIAN-TURNIP.

Arisaema triphyllum. Arum Family.

Scape. — Terminated by a hood-like leaf or spathe. *Leaves.* — Generally two; each divided into three leaflets. *Flowers.* — Small and inconspicuous; packed about the lower part of the fleshy spike or spadix which is shielded by the spathe. *Fruit.* — A bright scarlet berry which is packed upon the spadix with many others.

These quaint little preachers, ensconced in their delicate pulpits, are well known to all who love the woods in early spring. Sometimes these "pulpits" are of a light green, veined with a deeper tint; again they are stained with purple. This difference in color has been thought to indicate the 'sex of the flowers within — the males are said to be shielded by the green, the females by the purple, hoods. In the nearly allied cuckoo-pints of England, matters appear to be reversed: these plants are called "Lords and Ladies" by the children, the purple-tinged ones being the "Lords," the light green ones the "Ladies." The generic name, *Arisaema,* signifies *bloody arum,* and refers to the dark purple stains of the spathe. An old legend claims that these were received at the Crucifixion:

> "Beneath the cross it grew;
> And in the vase-like hollow of the leaf,
> Catching from that dread shower of agony
> A few mysterious drops, transmitted thus
> Unto the groves and hills their healing stains,
> A heritage, for storm or vernal shower
> Never to blow away."

The Indians were in the habit of boiling the bright scarlet berries which are so conspicuous in our autumn woods and devouring them with great relish; they also discovered that the bulb-like base, or *corm,* as it is called, lost its acridity on cooking, and made nutritious food, winning for the plant its name of Indian-turnip. One of its more local titles is memory-root, which it owes to a favorite schoolboy trick of tempting others to bite into the blistering corm with results likely to create a memorable impression.

The English cuckoo-pint yielded a starch which was greatly valued in the time of Elizabethan ruffs, although it proved too blistering to the hands of the washerwomen to remain long in use. Owing to the profusion with which the plant grows in Ireland efforts have been made to utilize it as food in periods of scarcity. By grating the corm into water, and then pouring off the liquid and drying the sediment, it is said that a tasteless, but nutritious, powder can be procured.

SKUNK CABBAGE. SWAMP CABBAGE.

Symplocarpus foetidus. Arum Family.

Leaves. — Large; becoming one or two feet long; heart-shaped, appearing later than the purple-mottled spathe and hidden flowers. *Flowers.* — Small and inconspicuous; packed on the fleshy spike which is hidden within the spathe.

If we are bold enough to venture into certain swampy places in the leafless woods and brown cheerless meadows of March, we notice that the sharply pointed spathes of the skunk cabbage have already pierced the surface of the earth. Until I chanced upon a passage in Thoreau's journal under date of October 31st, I had supposed that these "hermits of the bog" were only encouraged to make their appearance by the advent of those first balmy, spring-suggestive days which occasionally occur as early as February. But it seems that many of these young buds had pushed their way upward before the winter set in, for Thoreau counsels those who are afflicted with the melancholy of autumn to go to the swamps, "and see the brave spears of skunk cabbage buds already advanced toward a new year." "Mortal and human creatures must take a little respite in this fall of the year," he writes. "Their spirits do flag a little. There is a little questioning of destiny, and thinking to go like cowards to where the weary shall be at rest. But not so with the skunk cabbage. Its withered leaves fall and are transfixed by a rising bud. Winter and death are ignored. The circle of life is complete. Are these false prophets? Is it a lie or a vain boast underneath the skunk-cabbage bud pushing it upward and lifting the dead leaves with it?"

The purplish shell-like leaf, which curls about the tiny flowers which are thus hidden from view, is a rather grewsome-looking object, suggestive of a great snail when it lifts itself fairly above its muddy bed. When one sees it grouped with brother-cabbages it is easy to understand why a nearly allied species, which abounds along the Italian Riviera, should be entitled "Cappucini" by the neighboring peasants, for the bowed, hooded appearance of these plants might easily suggest the cowled Capuchins.

It seems unfortunate that our earliest spring flower (for such it undoubtedly is) should possess so unpleasant an odor as to win for itself the unpoetic title of skunk cabbage. There is also some incongruity in the heading of the great floral procession of the year by the minute hidden blossoms of this plant. That they are enabled to survive the raw March winds which are rampant when they first appear is probably due to the protection afforded them by the leathery leaf or spathe. When the true leaves unfold they mark the wet woods and meadows with bright patches of rich foliage, which with that of the hellebore, flash constantly into sight as we travel through the country in April.

It is interesting to remember that the skunk cabbage is nearly akin to the spotless calla-lily, the purple-mottled spathe of the one

SKUNK CABBAGE *Symplocarpus foetidus*

answering to the snowy petal-like leaf of the other. Meehan* tells us that the name bear-weed was given to the plant by the early Swedish settlers in the neighborhood of Philadelphia. It seems that the bears greatly relished this early green, which Meehan remarks "must have been a hot morsel, as the juice is acrid, and is said to possess some narcotic power, while that of the root, when chewed, causes the eyesight to grow dim."

WILD GINGER.

Asarum canadense. Birthwort Family.

Leaves. — One or two on each plant; kidney or heart-shaped; fuzzy; long-stalked. *Flowers.* — Dull purplish-brown; solitary; close to the ground on a short flower-stalk from the fork of the leaves.

Certain flowers might be grouped under the head of "vegetable cranks." Here would be classed the evening-primrose, which only opens at night, the closed gentian, which never opens at all, and the wild ginger, whose odd, unlovely flower seeks protection beneath its long-stemmed fuzzy leaves, and hides its head upon the ground as if unwilling to challenge comparison with its more brilliant brethren. Unless already familiar with this plant there is nothing to tell one when it has reached its flowering season; and many a wanderer through the rocky woods in early May quite overlooks its shy, shamefaced blossom.

The ginger-like flavor of the rootstock is responsible for its common name. It grows wild in many parts of Europe and is cultivated in England, where at one time it was considered a remedy for headache and deafness.

CARRION-FLOWER.

Smilax herbacea. Lily Family.

Stem. — Climbing, three to fifteen feet high. *Leaves.* — Ovate, or rounded heart-shaped, or abruptly cut off at base. *Flowers.* — Greenish or yellowish; small; clustered. *Fruit.* — A bluish-black berry.

---

*Thomas Meehan, American botanist (1826–1901).

WILD GINGER
Asarum canadense

CARRION-FLOWER
Smilax herbacea

Single staminate flower

Fruit

One whiff of the foul breath of the carrion-flower suffices for its identification. Thoreau likens its odor to that of "a dead rat in the wall." It seems unfortunate that this strikingly handsome plant, which clambers so ornamentally over the luxuriant thickets which border our lanes and streams, should be so handicapped each June. Happily with the disappearance of the blossoms, it takes its place as one of the most attractive of our climbers.

The common greenbrier, *S. rotundifolia,* is a near relation which is easily distinguished by its prickly stem.

The dark berries and deeply tinted leaves of this genus add greatly to the glorious autumnal display along our roadsides and in the woods and meadows.

GROUNDNUT. WILD BEAN.

Apios americana. Pea Family.

Stem. — Twining and climbing over bushes. *Leaves.* — Divided into three to seven narrowly oval leaflets. *Flowers.* — Purplish or chocolate-color, somewhat violet-scented; closely clustered in racemes.

In late summer the dark, rich flowers of the wild bean are found in short, thick clusters among the luxuriant undergrowth and thickets of low ground. The plant is a climber, bearing edible pear-shaped tubers on underground shoots, which give it its generic name signifying *a pear.*

WILD BEAN *Apios americana*

INDEX

Page numbers in *italic* refer to line drawings; page numbers in **bold** refer to color plates.

Rhododendron maximum, 36–37
Rhododendron nudiflorum, 31,
    179–81
Rhododendron viscosum, 30, 63
Robin-Run-Away, 49
Robinson, William, 91
Rocket, Yellow, 100
Rose-Mallow, 198–99, 199,
    203; Swamp, 198–99
Rubus odoratus, 103, 186, 187
Rudbeckia hirta, 125, 125, 215
Rue-anemone, 6, 6, 43
Ruskin, John, 38

Sabatia stellaris, 196–98, 203
Sagittaria latifolia, 86, 87, 123
St. Johnswort
    Common, 116–17, 117
    Marsh, 200, 201, 203
Salmon, William, 40
Sambucus canadensis, 63, 66
Sanguinaria canadensis, 3, 7
Saponaria officinalis, 163, 206
Sarracenia purpurea, 220–21
Saxifraga virginiensis, 11, 19
Saxifrage, Early, 11, 11, 19
Scabious, Sweet, 65
Scarlet Pimpernel, 163, 224,
    224
Scutellaria, 236, 237
Sea-Lavender, 203, 247, 247
Sea-Pink, 196–98, 197, 203
Selfheal, 83, 246, 246
Serviceberry, 3–4
Shadbush, 3–4, 31
Shakespeare, William, 196,
    238

Shinleaf, 39–40, 39, 103
Sidesaddle-Flower, 220–21
Silene caroliniana var.
    pensylvanica, 103, 160,
    161
Silverrod, 141, 142
Simpler's-Joy, 242–44
Sisyrinchium angustifolium, 215,
    228–29
Sium suave, 63, 69
Skullcap, 236, 237
Skunk Cabbage, 7, 270–72,
    271
Smilacina racemosa, 24–25, 83
Smilax herbacea, 103, 272–74
Snake-Mouth, 173–74
Snakeroot
    Black, 46
    White, 80, 80, 171
Snowberry, Creeping, 15
Soapwort, 206
Solanum dulcamara, 231, 250–
    51
Solidago, 140–42, 143
Solomon's Seal, 97, 97, 259
    False, 24, 25, 83
Sorrel, Wood-, 37–38, 38,
    103
Spatterdock, 122, 123
Spiraea latifolia, 60, 183
Spiranthes cernua, 86–87
Sprengel, Christian Konrad,
    233
Spring-Beauty, 7, 43, 157–59,
    159
Squirrel-Corn, 15, 259
Starflower, 9, 9

Violet
Canada, 22–23, *23*, **31**
Common Blue, 238–41
Dog's-Tooth-, 92–93
Downy Yellow, 100, *101*,
259
Lance-leaved, 23, **31**
Sweet White, 22, **31**
Viper's Bugloss, **111**, 248–49
Virginia Cowslip, 266
Virgin's-Bower, 76, *76*, **231**

Wakerobin, 7, 210–11
Wallace, Alfred, 266
Water-Arum, 28
Watercress, 12, **123**
Water-Hemlock, 69, **215**
Water-Lily, Fragrant, 88, **123**

Water-Parsnip, **63**, 69
Whip-Poor-Will Shoe, 108
White-Hearts, 14–15
Whiteweed, 50
Whittier, John Greenleaf, 4,
156–57
Willow-Herb, Great, 194
Windflower, 4–5
Winter Cress, 100, *101*
Wintergreen, 29, *29*
One-flowered, 33, *33*, **83**
Witch Hazel, 145–46, *145*,
239
Wood-Sorrel, 37–38, *38*, **103**
Wordsworth, William, 98–99

Yarrow, Common, 68–69, *68*,
71